# N E T
# curriculum

An Educator's Guide To Using The Internet

# NET
# curriculum

An Educator's Guide To Using The Internet

## by Linda C. Joseph

CyberAge Books

**Information Today, Inc.**
Medford, New Jersey

*Net Curriculum: An Educator's Guide to Using the Internet*

**Library of Congress Cataloging-in-Publication Data**

Joseph, Linda C., 1949-
   Net curriculum : an educator's guide to using the Internet / by Linda C. Joseph.
      p.       cm.
   Includes index.
   ISBN 0-910965-30-7 (pbk.)
   1. Teaching--Computer network resources.    2. Education--Computer network resources
3. Internet (Computer network) in education.
I. Title.
LB1044.87.J67    1999
371.33'44678--dc21                              98-43723
                                                      CIP

Printed and bound in the United States of America.

Cover Design: Face-Up Design
Book Design: Patricia F. Kirkbride
Index: Laurie Andriot

# Table of Contents

**Foreword** ................................................................................................ ix
*by Susan Veccia*

**Acknowledgments** .................................................................................. xiii

**Introduction** .......................................................................................... xv

**Chapter 1: Cyberspace Research—Working the Web** ........................ 1
  THE BIG6 APPROACH ............................................................................ 1
    The Big6 Skills ............................................................................... 1
    Lesson Plan .................................................................................... 3
    Big6 Assignment Organizer ........................................................... 14
  WEBQUEST APPROACH ......................................................................... 16
    America Dreams ............................................................................. 16
  CITING ELECTRONIC RESOURCES ......................................................... 16
    Style Guides for Citing Electronic Resources ............................... 17
  CYBERGUIDE RATINGS ........................................................................ 
    WWW CyberGuide Ratings for Content Evaluation ...................... 19
  WHAT DO YOU SEE? .......................................................................... 22

**Chapter 2: Internet Resources** ......................................................... 25
  GENERAL SITES .................................................................................. 25
  ART SITES .......................................................................................... 27
  CLIP ART SITES .................................................................................. 29
  ECONOMICS SITES .............................................................................. 29
  ENCYCLOPEDIA SITES ......................................................................... 30
  FOREIGN LANGUAGE SITES ................................................................. 30
  HEALTH AND NUTRITION SITES .......................................................... 31
  KEYPALS ............................................................................................ 32
  LANGUAGE ARTS SITES ...................................................................... 32
  MATH SITES ....................................................................................... 35
  MUSIC SITES ...................................................................................... 38
  PHYSICAL EDUCATION SITES .............................................................. 39
  SCIENCE SITES ................................................................................... 39
  SOCIAL STUDIES SITES ....................................................................... 45

African Americans ———————————————————————— 45
Biography ———————————————————————————— 47
Civil War —————————————————————————————— 48
Geography ————————————————————————————— 49
Government ————————————————————————————— 50
Immigration —————————————————————————————— 52
Law —————————————————————————————————— 52
History ————————————————————————————————— 52
Multicultural ———————————————————————————— 54
Native Americans ————————————————————————— 54
Westward Expansion —————————————————————— 55
Women ———————————————————————————————— 59
**STUDY AND RESEARCH SITES** ———————————————— 59

# Chapter 3: Internet Project Ideas and Activities

## Chapter 3: Internet Project Ideas and Activities ———— 61
**STARTING POINTS** ————————————————————————— 61
**PROJECT SAMPLES** —————————————————————————— 63
**SEND A WEB POSTCARD** ——————————————————— 64
**JUST FOR FUN!** ————————————————————————————— 66
**LANGUAGE ARTS ACTIVITY IDEAS** —————————————— 68
Reach Out and Touch an Author ————————————————— 68
Pop-Up Books ——————————————————————————— 71
Unleash Creative Talents ———————————————————— 72
**MATH ACTIVITY IDEAS** ———————————————————————— 74
Bubble Geometry ————————————————————————— 74
M&M Math ————————————————————————————— 75
**SCIENCE ACTIVITY IDEAS** —————————————————————— 76
Flying Free—Paper Airplane Science ——————————————— 76
Space ... the Final Frontier—Land Rovers on the Move ———— 77
Additional Space Web Sites ————————————————————— 77
Schoolyard Science—Making a Weather Station ——————— 78
Rain Forest Music ————————————————————————— 80
Schoolyard Science—Design a Butterfly Garden ——————— 81
**SOCIAL STUDIES ACTIVITY IDEAS** ——————————————— 82
Country Journey ————————————————————————— 82
Culture Capsule ——————————————————————————— 83
Here Come the Cybercasters ————————————————————— 83
Some Additional Suggestions ————————————————————— 83
**READY REFERENCE SCAVENGER HUNT** ———————————— 85
**BELLS AND WHISTLES ON THE WEB** —————————————— 87

# Chapter 4: Copyright and Property Rights _____ 89
COPYRIGHT AND FAIR USE REFERENCES _____ 89
WEB BUDDY _____ 90
WEB WHACKER _____ 91
OFF-LINE CAPTURING USING NETSCAPE COMMUNICATOR 4.0 ____ 91

# Chapter 5: Acceptable Use and Student Safety ___ 97
ACCEPTABLE USE _____ 97
    Nancy Willard's K-12 Acceptable Use Policy _____ 98
KEEPING KIDS SAFE _____ 105
    Keeping Kids Safe in the World of Technology _____ 105

# Appendix A: Getting Connected _____ 109
INTERNET CONNECTION _____ 109
    America Online _____ 111
    Dial-Up PPP _____ 111
    ISDN _____ 112
    LAN/WAN _____ 113
    Cable Modem _____ 114
FUTURE OPTIONS _____ 114
    ADSL _____ 114
    MMDS _____ 115
INTERNET CLIENT SOFTWARE PROGRAMS _____ 115
    Shareware and Freeware _____ 116
    Plug-Ins _____ 118
SETTING UP A PPP CONNECTION—WINDOWS 95 _____ 120
    Configuring the "Network" Control Panel _____ 120
    Configuring Dial-Up Networking _____ 122
    Creating a Connection to Your Internet Service Provider ___ 123
    Logging On to the Internet _____ 126
SETTING UP A PPP CONNECTION—MACINTOSH _____ 126
    Setting Up the Modem _____ 127
    Config PPP Setup _____ 127
    Setting Up TCP/IP Open Transport _____ 130
    Logging On to the Internet _____ 131

# Appendix B: Accessing Information _____ 133
E-MAIL _____ 133
    Sending an E-Mail Message _____ 134

Signature File .................................................... 137
Attachments ..................................................... 137
**ELECTRONIC DISCUSSION GROUPS** ................... 138
Joining a Listserv Electronic Discussion Group .... 139
Posting a Message ............................................ 139
Leaving a Listserv Discussion Group ................... 140
**NEWSGROUPS** ............................................... 140
**WORLD WIDE WEB** .......................................... 141
**TELNET** ......................................................... 142
Telnet Step-by-Step Instructions ....................... 144
**FTP** ............................................................. 144
FTP Step-by-Step Instructions for Downloading ... 145
FTP Step-by-Step Instructions for Uploading ....... 146
Compression Utility Programs ............................ 148
**NEWS STREAMING** ......................................... 149
**TELECONFERENCING** ...................................... 151

**Appendix C: Electronic Publishing** ............ 155
**TIPS FOR GETTING STARTED** ........................... 155
Some Good Sources for Web Publishing ............. 155
**GUIDE FOR MAKING A SCHOOL HOME PAGE** ..... 156
Design Elements .............................................. 156
Content ......................................................... 157
Before You Begin ............................................. 157
Ten Tips for Webmasters ................................... 158
Design Tools ................................................... 158
**HTML** .......................................................... 160
Beginning and Ending Tags ............................... 160
Image Tag ...................................................... 161
Headers and Line Breaks .................................. 163
Adding Links to Your School Page ...................... 164
Adding Background Colors ................................ 167
Tables ........................................................... 168
**HOME PAGE TEMPLATE** ................................. 169
HTML Tags ..................................................... 173

**Appendix D: Glossary** ............................... 175

**Index A: Subjects** ...................................... 179

**Index B: Web Sites** .................................... 187

# Foreword

I am sitting in my son's living room in Jacksonville, Florida, reading an e-mail message from him 400 miles off the coast of California. He is on board the *U.S.S. Stennis*, returning from six months in the Persian Gulf. Tomorrow, he and other Naval aviators will take off from the carrier and fly nonstop to the East Coast, culminating in a dramatic "fly-by" before landing in Jacksonville. I'm a good mom. I want to be there when he lands—and, of course, see his airplane scream by in a close formation with the other returning planes. His e-mail message gives me the latest information on Hurricane Bonnie forming in the Caribbean and the news that Bonnie is expected to head north and thus will not change their flight plans. I can go about my plans for the day knowing that I need to be back by late afternoon.

I am also trying to squeeze as much as I can out of the day, so as I wait, I'm searching the Net to find information about buying a new car—a task I don't relish. I find the **www.edmunds.com** and other automotive Web sites and I wonder if I will be so brave as to actually place an order online. As I think about this, I remember that I bought my airline ticket to Jacksonville over the Web, and got a much better price than I did when I called the airline directly, so I'm thinking … hmmm. Maybe I really *can* use the Web to buy a car! I send an e-mail message to my office at the Library of Congress about an appointment I have on Friday, and then I am free for the rest of the day until the appointed hour arrives.

I am a technology neophyte and I absolutely hate machines, yet *information technology* plays a central role in my life. Not that we are joined at the hip, but I find it hard to imagine life without a computer and modem. It is so convenient. So efficient. For our children, knowing how to use a "connected computer" as a *communication device* is a vital life skill. We must do more than pay lip service to the need to teach information literacy skills in our nation's schools. We must help educators get up to speed on new technologies. This is hard for teachers or school media specialists who do not always have as much access to training as do other professionals. Linda Joseph's book provides educators with a helpful "getting started" resource that they will want to chain to their computers!

No one is better qualified to write an Internet "desktop reference" for educators than Linda Joseph. Linda has scoured the Net for years on what seems like a constant quest for rich, reliable and … yes … even entertaining online resources that complement K-12 curricula. Linda understands both teachers and kids and pulls together a compendium of incredibly helpful tips and tricks. Linda also understands that most of us do not learn in a vacuum. We learn best when we have a need to know, for whatever reason.

In the pages of this book, Linda provides not only examples of the "best" of the Web, but does so within the context of teaching information access skills in K-12 schools. "Surfing" is not "searching." Knowing how to find, access, and evaluate information is a critical life skill—one that needs to be taught every day in our nation's schools and public libraries. Linda provides several useful frameworks for teaching information literacy, plus she provides a quick "cookbook" approach to getting started.

I have learned so much from Linda since we first met in 1995. In the fall of 1994, I decided to take on the risky proposition of launching a magazine about school information technology. As founding editor of *MultiMedia Schools*, my first challenge was to tap into the expertise that already existed in K-12 schools nationwide. I had loads of experience with traditional online searching and a good handle on electronic products and services. But, I was less comfortable with the Internet and how it was being used in schools. I began by lurking on listservs and attending as many technology conferences as I could.

Ironically, one of the first conferences I attended was Computers in Libraries in March of 1995. I sat down for coffee with a marketing representative from one of the major databanks to talk about his view of school technology. In the course of that meeting, being a chatty person, he introduced me to customers as they happened by. And that's when my personal network of super sharp school librarians began to take shape. Who's the best person to write a technical but readable "how-to" Internet column for K-12 educators?, I asked. One person from Richmond, Virginia, and another from Columbus, Ohio, chanted in unison, "Linda Joseph!"

I heard all the stories about Linda's amazing feats. How she began to share her knowledge with others through various professional development workshops in her own school district and then later throughout the nation. How she kept dozens of plates spinning at the same time, presenting at conferences, writing a newsletter, and even publishing (in 1995) an Internet "how-to" book entitled *World Link*, while she held down a full-time job as a media specialist in the Columbus Public School System.

I resolved to meet this superwoman, but felt sure that she would be "too busy" to do any work specifically for *MultiMedia Schools*. That hastily formed conclusion proved just how much I had to learn about Linda Joseph. As she chattered about various projects and ideas, I was stretching my imagination to figure out a way to harness this bundle of energy. Out of this conversation emerged "CyberBee," the Internet column that since September, 1996, has run in each issue of *MultiMedia Schools* magazine (**http://www.infotoday.com/MMSchools**).

In the CyberBee column, Linda has written on American Indians, art projects, dinosaurs, math games, science fairs, and social studies themes. The list goes on and on. It is a delight to work with Linda because she is not only knowledgeable about "technical" things, but she is focused on the learner, whether that person is a child, a teacher, a colleague, or a parent. She is practical. She will tell you what you need to know when you need to know it. She is a good writer who can make complex things seem simple. And, finally, she is a seasoned professional who sets her own bar very high. Fact checking, a tedious but necessary editorial function, is never an issue with Linda. She does careful, accurate work—always.

I now know Linda both as a friend and a colleague, and I have learned my lessons well. She has been my Internet mentor; perhaps she will be yours, too.

—Susan Veccia

*Susan Veccia is a librarian and project manager for the Library of Congress National Digital Library Program. Through this program, resources from the American Memory online collections are being used by K-12 school teachers and librarians. Prior to joining the National Digital Library, Susan chaired the 1991-1992 American Memory User Evaluation, which tested the prototype system in 44 schools and public libraries nationwide. In previous years, she has worked for the Library of Congress Congressional Research Service as an online trainer and system design specialist.*

*In addition to her 18 years' work at the Library of Congress, Susan was the founding editor of* MultiMedia Schools, *a national magazine that addresses the practical concerns of teachers and librarians working with new technologies. She has judged the Software Publishers Association Best Educational Software Codies Award and currently serves on the National Advisory Board of ERIC.*

# Acknowledgments

Linda Resch and Karen Schwab, my good friends.

My publisher, Tom Hogan, Sr., and my editors, John Bryans and Dorothy Pike. Also at Information Today, Inc., Heide Dengler, Patricia F. Kirkbride, Heather Rudolph, and Tom Hogan, Jr.

Susan Veccia, for the Foreword.

Darlene Vanasco, Face Up Design, for the cover art.

Dr. Michael Eisenberg for permission to use the Big6 chart, definitions, and lesson plan form.

Barbara Janson for permission to use the Big6 Organizer.

Karen McLachlan for permission to use the WWW CyberGuide form.

The Library of Congress (National Digital Library) for permission to use the photo analysis guide.

Nancy Willard for permission to use the Acceptable Use Policy template.

Linda Uhrenholt for permission to use "Keeping Kids Safe."

# Introduction

Within the last few years, the Internet has evolved into a major resource for teachers and students. How can we successfully integrate the resources available on the Internet into classrooms or library media centers? What strategies can we use with students to help them become better navigators and informed consumers? What skills do our students need to effectively utilize the Internet? Throughout this book, these questions and more are answered.

To educators wanting to use these strategies and resources, I offer these suggestions. Visit outstanding Web sites. Explore dozens of projects and activities that you can use immediately in your own program. Incorporate problem-based learning utilizing the Big6 Information Access Skills or WebQuests. Learn how to evaluate Web sites and cite electronic resources. Experiment with different search engines to find the information you need. Determine what is fair use and what resources are protected by copyright. Examine the guidelines for developing an Acceptable Use Policy and how to introduce Kid Safety on the Internet to students and parents.

In the appendices of this book you will find nuts and bolts information that will be more or less useful to you depending on your level of experience using the Internet. There are step-by-step instructions here for getting connected, accessing information on the Net, finding and using freeware and shareware programs, and creating a home page (including an easy-to-use home page template). A glossary and index round out the book.

Although there are dozens of Web sites listed, this is not meant to be a definitive list, but merely starting points for those beginning their journey down the information superhighway. Much of the material in this book was created for educational workshops. So you might say that this book has been test-driven and used many times in real-world situations.

As the CyberBee columnist for *MultiMedia Schools* magazine, I write about how the Web can be used in many curriculum areas. The CyberBee Web site is a place where you can find additional tie-ins and up-to-date hyperlinks to all of the sites listed in the magazine articles as well as in this book.

You are invited to fly with CyberBee on fantastic Internet adventures. Your itinerary includes tips, curriculum ideas, cool Web sites, scavenger hunts, and step-by-step guides for using technology. Book your flight now and let CyberBee show you how to harness the power and energy of the Internet as you guide students through engaged learning activities that expand their knowledge and their technological skills.

**http://www.cyberbee.com**

# Chapter 1

# Cyberspace Research— Working the Web

## THE BIG6 APPROACH

**http://big6.syr.edu**

Teaching information access skills cannot be done in a vacuum. It must relate to the learning environment by actively engaging students to gather and process information in a meaningful way. For example, a lesson using a magazine index is soon forgotten if students are not involved in a related activity. Teaching the same lesson while students are working on a project brings the lesson to life. Students now understand that learning how to use the magazine index will help them find information about their chosen topic and successfully complete the project. The process teaches them important critical thinking and problem solving skills, and the same is true when they use the Internet. However, surfing can be frustrating and time consuming. So where do we begin in order to use this vast resource?

Put the project into the context of the Big6 Skills, an approach to information problem solving developed by Michael B. Eisenberg and Robert E. Berkowitz. In this systematic method, Eisenberg and Berkowitz define six steps for resolving the initial problem.

## The Big6 Skills

*(The sidebar presenting the Big6 Skills (see next page) has been reproduced with permission from Eisenberg, M.B. and Berkowitz, R.E., Information Problem*

# The Big6 Skills

1. Task Definition:  determining the need for information
2. Information Seeking Strategies:   examining alternative approaches to acquiring the appropriate information to meet defined tasks
3. Location and Access:  locating information sources and information within sources
4. Use of Information:  using a source to gain information
5. Synthesis:  integrating information drawn from a range of sources
6. Evaluation:  making judgments based on a set of criteria

## Information Problem Solving Using the Big6 Skills

1. Task Definition:
    1.1 Define the problem.
    1.2 Identify information requirements of the problem.
2. Information Seeking Strategies:
    2.1 Determine the range of possible sources.
    2.2 Evaluate the different possible sources to determine priorities.
3. Location and Access:
    3.1 Locate sources.
    3.2 Find information within sources.
4. Use of Information:
    4.1 Engage (e.g., read, hear, view) the information in a source.
    4.2 Extract relevant information from a source.
5. Synthesis:
    5.1 Organize information from multiple sources.
    5.2 Present information.
6. Evaluation:
    6.1 Judge the result (effectiveness).
    6.2 Judge the information problem-solving process (efficiency).

## The Big6 in Question Form:

1. What needs to be done?
2. What can I use to find what I need?
3. Where can I find what I need?
4. What information can I use?
5. How can I put my information together?
6. How will I know if I did my job well?

## For younger students you may want to use the Super 3:

1. A Beginning
2. A Middle
3. An End

## ► Tip

To subscribe to the Big6 LISTSERV, send an e-mail message to listserv.syr.edu. Leave the subject line blank. In the text of your message, enter the following: SUB BIG6 followed by your first name and last name.

*Solving: The Big6 Skills Approach to Library & Information Skills Instruction, Norwood, NJ: Ablex Publishing Corporation, 1990, p. 24.)*

How can the Internet be used as one of the tools in this process? To answer this question, let's take the topic "Environmental Habitats" and go through the Big6 process using the Internet. Think about correlating e-mail with writing skills and social interaction. Develop information gathering skills using the Web. When students process the information by critically reading, viewing, and listening, it helps them determine what materials are useful to solve a problem or answer a question. By sharing their reports and projects with others, students will gain valuable feedback for future learning.

Within this context you become the facilitator and your students become collaborators with their peers. Not only will they learn valuable problem solving skills, but how to work together for common solutions. This helps prepare them to be world citizens in an information society.

After working through the process, the next step is to construct a lesson plan.

## Lesson Plan

*(The sample lesson plan* (see next page) *has been reproduced with the permission of Michael B. Eisenberg and Robert E. Berkowitz, from the* Resource Companion to Curriculum Initiative: An Agenda and Strategy for Library Media Programs. *In this example, the study of animal habitat is adapted to the matrix of the Big6 Skills.)*

# LESSON PLAN

Date:

Subject:  Science, Interdisciplinary

Teacher:

Class:

Lesson Name:  Animal Habitat

Location:

Time: 3-4 weeks

Unit Context:  Current Environmental Issues Between Man and Nature

Content Objectives:

The student will be able to:

1. Recognize and identify the importance of animal habitat and adaptation on survival

2. Understand the impact of the industrial society on wildlife

| **Big6 Skills Objectives:** | **Activities:** |
| --- | --- |
| 1. Task: | 1. Student Groups formed. General discussion for research |
| 2. Information seeking: | 2. List information available—be sure to include several types of media. |
| 3. Location: | 3. Library, local wildlife conservation facility, Internet: To include observation and inquiry. |
| 4. Use of Information: | 4. Examine resources from Internet, CD-ROM, books, magazine index; observe wildlife habitat at conservation site. |
| 5. Synthesis: | 5. Each student contributes his/her research to be included in the presentation. Each group will create a chart of the characteristics of its animal's habitat in ClarisWorks |
| 6. Evaluation: | 6. Each group is responsible for a ten-minute recap of its findings to share with the entire class. A choice of notebook or multimedia project will be required of each group. |

Materials/Resources:  Animal Encyclopedias, Books on Animal Habitats, Wild America Videos, Internet (e-mail scientists with questions, retrieve pictures, articles, read listservs on the topic), and visit a wildlife conservation facility.

Evaluation:  Self evaluation, peer review, and teacher

Notes:  Each student will contribute his or her component to make a complete overview of animal habitat. The entire group makes an oral presentation to the class. The notebook or multimedia project will receive a group grade.

# Using the Big6 to Search the Web

Using the broad topic "environmental habitats of animals," we will go through the six steps and see how they relate to the Internet.

## *Big6 # 1: Task Definition*

Step 1 is to determine the need for information. This is the point where you will define the problem you want to solve or the question you want to answer.

- Choose a General Area for Study (we've chosen environmental habitats of animals)

- Narrow the Subject (for instance, to specific animals such as whales, kangaroos, polar bears, pandas, elephants, etc.)

- Define the Question(s) You Want to Answer or Explore (for instance, where does your animal live? What is the climate like? What kind of food does your animal eat?)

- Think of Keywords or Phrases (for instance, "animal habitats," "panda habitats," "animal food," "zoos," etc.)

## *Big6 #2: Information Seeking*

Step 2 can be a brainstorming session to think of all the places you might go to find resources that will help you answer your questions (for instance, natural history museums, CD-ROMs, books, interviews with naturalists, Web resources).

## *Big6 #3: Location and Access*

In Step 3, you will locate the sources and begin searching for information. On the Web, you will want to try different search engines and starting points. Sometimes, you will simply stumble onto information by chance.

### Search Engines

Each search engine indexes its own list of Web sites. They may be updated on a daily, weekly, or monthly basis. Search engines such as AltaVista, Electric Library, and Infoseek use different strategies and procedures for searching. You will want to look at the directions and tips at each site for complete details. Be sure to check The Internet Search Tools Quick Reference Guide. You can print out a handy search chart to keep next to your computer. It was designed by the Instructional Technology Resource Center in Florida (http://www.itrc.ucf.edu/iqr/).

***Boolean—using the connectors AND, OR.*** AltaVista (http://www.altavista. com) AltaVista also allows you to search by phrase or natural language. When using a natural language search, you may get hits that have no relevance to what you want.

(Boolean) Type: *panda and habitat*

**FIGURE 1.1 Searching AltaVista using Boolean language**

***Natural Language.*** Electric Library (http://www.elibrary.com) Electric Library allows you to ask questions and select what type of resources you want to retrieve. Although it is a subscription service, it is one of the best sources for finding information and pictures.

Two other terrific sites for searching by natural language are Ask Jeeves (http://www.askjeeves.com/) and Ask Jeeves for Kids (http:///www.ajkids.com/). This is a fast and easy way to find information because this site has created a database of six million answers to the most popular questions. It also provides a "metasearch" option.

(Natural Language) Try typing: *What do pandas eat?*

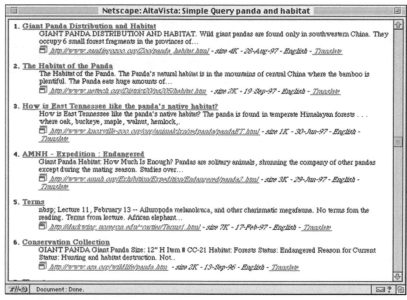

**FIGURE 1.2   *Searching AltaVista using Natural Language***

(Natural Language) Check the boxes for pictures, magazines, books, and newspapers. Then type this question: Where do pandas live?

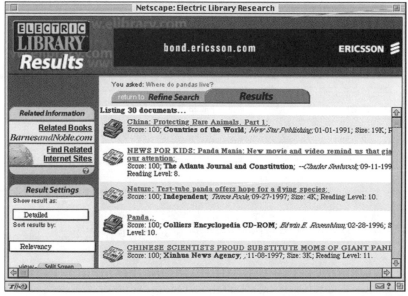

**FIGURE 1.3   *Searching Electric Library using Natural Language.***

(Natural Language) If you want a picture of a panda, simply check the picture box and type: *panda.*

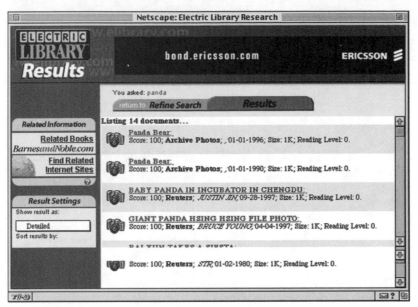

**FIGURE 1.4    Searching Electric Library, cont.**

*Keyword.* Infoseek (http://www.infoseek.com) allows you to find information by keyword or phrase.

| A search for... | Returns pages containing... |
| --- | --- |
| panda habitat | panda or habitat |
| +panda habitat | panda, maybe habitat |
| "panda habitat" | The word panda next to the word habitat |

(Keyword) Next type: *+panda +habitat* (See Figure 1.5)

(Keyword) Type: *"panda habitat"* (See Figure 1.6)

Print the first page of each search and compare the results.

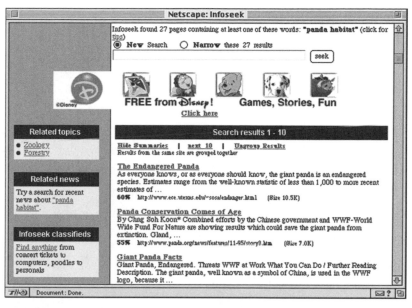

*FIGURE 1.5   Searching Infoseek using keywords*

*FIGURE 1.6   Searching Infoseek, cont.*

## Kid Safe Search Engines

Yahooligans is a directory of subject areas for browsing and searching.
Magellan allows you to search green light sites that have been reviewed.

Yahooligans
http://www.yahooligans.com

Magellan
http://www.mckinley.com

## Searching Multiple Engines

Beyond individual search engines, multiple engines can be used. MetaCrawler and other "meta-search engines" let you query several search engines at one time. They retrieve the top hits by relevancy. This can be a time-saver. However, there are occasions where sites are duplicated several times or useful information is not retrieved. Experiment and see how it works for you.

MetaCrawler
http://www.metacrawler.com

## Starting Points

Starting points are places where specific topics have been searched and links created. Many include annotations describing the Web site. Compare these two sites:

NetVet—The Electronic Zoo
http://netvet.wustl.edu/ssi.htm

ZooNet
http://www.mindspring.com/~zoonet/

## Lucky Finds

Sometimes you will simply find an interesting Web site without searching. The Ohio Wildlife Division sets up a live cam on top of the Rhodes Tower in Columbus, Ohio, each spring when the falcons nest. It is fascinating to watch the hatching and growing process. This is an example of one of my lucky finds (see Figure 1.7).

Nesting Falcons Downtown Columbus, Ohio—Ohio Division of Wildlife
http://www.dnr.state.oh.us/odnr/wildlife/

## Ask An Expert

Asking experts questions is an excellent way to find information on specific topics.

ICONnect: KidsConnect
http://www.ala.org/ICONN/kidsconn.html

*FIGURE 1.7 Web site of nesting falcons.*

KidsConnect is an outstanding organization of volunteer librarians who point students to possible sources that will answer their questions. The response to a question is provided within forty-eight hours.

Pitsco's Ask An Expert

http://www.askanexpert.com/askanexpert

Pitsco's Ask an Expert Web site is a good starting point for locating individuals who will answer questions. However, be sure you know how each site operates in terms of the response time and the expertise of the individuals answering the questions.

## *Big6 #4: Use of Information*

In Step 4, ask these questions: How do you know the information is reliable? Can you use the photographs and music in projects without violating copyright? How do you cite resources?

### Evaluating and Selecting Content to Use in the Project

How do you know the information is reliable? Can you use the photographs and music in projects without violating copyright? How do you cite resources?

CyberGuides

http://www.cyberbee.com/guides.html

Compare the information at these two sites using the WWW CyberGuide Ratings for Content Evaluation by Karen McLachlan on page 20:

Giant Panda Facts

http://www.wwfcanada.org/facts/panda.html

The Habitat of the Panda

http://www.nettech.org/District20/ps205/habitat.htm

What were your results? Which site had the most reliable information?

## Selecting Content to Use in the Project

After evaluating the information at each Web site, students can create a folder of bookmarks of the pages that will provide the most reliable information.

## Citing Resources

Be sure to keep a record of the resources you are using for the report. It is important to give credit to the places where you found your information.

Citing a Web page

http://www.cyberbee.com/citing.html

Nueva School MLA Style Interactive Forms

http://www.nueva.pvt.k12.ca.us/~debbie/library/research/research.html

## *Big6 #5: Synthesis*

Step 5 is the culminating report or project. This can be anything from a written paper to a HyperStudio presentation to a reenactment. For examples of student projects and the resulting reports, check out the following Web resources:

Mr. Smith's Fifth Grade Research Reports—Oak View Elementary

http://oakview.fcps.edu/~smith/research

Join Us on a Prairie Tour—Happy Thought School, East Selkirk,
   Manitoba, Canada

http://198.163.125.130/imym/hts/hts.html

Student Use of Netscape as a Research Tool—Animals Around the World
http://www.chicojr.chico.k12.ca.us/staff/gray/isearch.html

## *Big6 #6: Evaluation*

The three parts to the evaluation process are self evaluation, peer evaluation, and teacher evaluation.

### Self Evaluation

A checklist might serve as a benchmark for students to determine for themselves whether or not they have met the criteria. See Step 6 of Barbara Jansen's Big6 Assignment Organizer on page 14 for an example.

Student Portfolios & Self-Assessment Rubrics, by Jim Askew
http://pc65.frontier.osrhe.edu/hs/science/ota4.htm

### Peer Evaluation

Peer evaluation might be accomplished through a series of sharing activities throughout the project. Small groups would meet and discuss their works in progress. This lends to a nonthreatening environment. For a global project you might have online discussions with other students who are also participating.

### Teacher Evaluation

In respect to teacher evaluation, ongoing comments as well as specific criteria or rubrics should be established.

Building Rubrics
http://www.sover.net/~mttop/arts/rubrics.html

Evaluating: Grading and Scoring
http://www.eduplace.com/rdg/res/ch11.html

### Use and Purpose of the Big6 Assignment Organizer

The Big6 Assignment Organizer (pages 14-15) will serve as a visual organizational tool for elementary and middle school students when they are working on an assignment. It will assist them in tracking their progress as well as provide them with a self-evaluation checklist.

# Big6 Assignment Organizer

Created by Barbara A. Jansen, this two-page handout leads students through the Big6 in clear language so they can successfully prepare for and complete assignments. Jansen keeps a stack of organizers in the library for students to take as needed and also gives out masters so teachers can provide copies when assigning projects.

The organizer is structured so that students complete steps one through five before beginning the assignment and step six before turning it in to their teacher. This version, for grades three through five, allows the student to plan an assignment independently or with parents. Teachers help the students fill in the Task Definition portion so there is no question about the assignment.

### Big6 #1:  Task Definition

Name: _____

Teacher: _____


Fill out Big6 #1-5 before you begin to work on your assignment. Fill out Big6 #6 before you turn your assignment in to your teacher.

What am I supposed to do? _____

_____

What information do I need in order to do this?

1. _____
2. _____
3. _____
4. _____
5. _____


### Big6 #2:  Information-Seeking Strategies

What are the possible sources to find this information? _____

_____

Which ones are best for me to use? _____


### Big6 #3:  Location and Access

Where will I find these sources? _____

_____

Who can help me find what I need? _____

_____

## Big6 Assignment Organizer *(cont.)*

### Big6 #4:  Use of Information

How will I record the information that I find?

_____ take notes using cards

_____ take notes on notebook paper

_____ take notes using a data chart

_____ draw pictures

_____ talk into a tape recorder

_____ other

How will I give credit to my sources?

_____ write title, author, page number on note cards

_____ write title, author, page number on notebook paper

_____ write title, author, page number on data chart

### Big6 #5: Synthesis

What product or performance will I make to finish my assignment? _____

_____

How will I give credit to my sources in my final product or performance?

_____ include a written list (bibliography)

_____ after the performance, tell which sources I used

_____ other _____

### Big6 #6:  Evaluation

How will I know that I have done my best?  (All must be checked before assignment is turned in.)

_____ what I made to finish the assignment is what I was supposed to do in #1

_____ information found in #4 matches information needed in #1

_____ I gave credit to my sources (even if I used a textbook)

_____ my work is neat

_____ my work is complete and includes my name and the date

# WEBQUEST APPROACH
**http://edweb.sdsu.edu/webquest/webquest.html**

WebQuest, another method for researching, was developed by Bernie Dodge at San Diego State University. The six building blocks for WebQuest include the introduction, task, process, resources, evaluation, and conclusion.

---

### Building Blocks for WebQuest

1. Introduction:    to orient the learner as to what is coming and raise some interest in the learner through a variety of means

2. Task:    what the learner will have done at the end of the exercise

3. Process:    steps that learners should go through in completing the task

4. Resources:    a list of Web pages which the instructor has located that will help the learner accomplish the task

5. Evaluation:    an evaluation rubric

6. Conclusion:    an opportunity to summarize the experience, to encourage reflection about the process, to extend and generalize what was learned

---

## America Dreams
**http://www.internet-catalyst.org/projects/amproject/toc.html**

An excellent example of a WebQuest is America Dreams (see Figure 1.8), an inquiry-based project developed to explore the American Memory Collection from the Library of Congress. From the convenience of your classroom, your students can sift through original source materials such as rare prints, sound recordings, and images, and learn about immigration at the turn of the century.

# CITING ELECTRONIC RESOURCES

As use of Internet resources by students has increased, the question being asked is, How do I cite this information in my reports? There are a number of

**FIGURE 1.8   The America Dreams Web page**

ways being circulated in print and on the Internet. It is important to cite the author, date (if known), title, source, medium, and how the information is available.

## Style Guides for Citing Electronic Resources

For more complete explanations about citing electronic resources, several Web sites offer guidance along with illustrative examples. Xia Li and Nancy B. Crane, authors of the book, *Electronic Styles: A Handbook for Citing Electronic Information* (Information Today, Inc. 1996), offer such information on their Web site.

Bibliographic Formats for Citing Electronic Information

http://www.uvm.edu/~ncrane/estyles/

The following examples are based on their book, which uses the APA and MLA styles, with additional features for electronic information.

*Example based on the APA Style:*

Hartman, Brian. (1996, July 9). Lamm To Seek Reform Party

Nomination. Now Politics [Online]. Available: http://www.politicsnow.
com/news/July96/09/pn0709lamm/index.htm [1996, July 9].

*Example based on the MLA Style:*

Hartman, Brian. "Lamm To Seek Reform Party Nomination." Now
Politics 9 July, 1996. Online. Available: http://www.politicsnow.com/
news/July96/ 09/pn0709lamm/index.htm. 9 July, 1996.

The next two resources also contain examples of APA and MLA styles for citing electronic resources, as well as discussion of the practice of citation in general and links to related sites.

Cybercitation in Hawaii's Schools
http://kalama.doe.hawaii.edu/hern95/rt007/
(Created by HERN95 Library Resource Team and Based on the MLA Style)

Electronic Style ... the Final Frontier
http://funnelweb.utcc.utk.edu/~hoemann/style.html

For a comprehensive discussion of styles and examples, the next Web site can
be highly informative. This Web site, compiled by Janice R. Walker, is endorsed
by the Alliance for Computers & Writing.

MLA-Style Citations of Electronic Sources
http://www.cas.usf.edu/english/walker/mla.html

The most practical and useful tool for citing references on the Web is an interactive form created by Debbie Abilock at the Nueva School Web site. Nueva
School MLA Style Interactive Forms http://www.nueva.pvt.k12.ca.us/~debbie/
library/research/research.html

First, follow the illustrated table to teach students what data they need to record
for their bibliography. Then have them type that information into the form and
click on the submit button. The reference will be returned in the proper format
ready to copy and paste into a word processing document. Citations are based on
the MLA style guide. The forms include an e-mail message, discussion group,
newsgroup, Web page, CD-ROM, book, magazine article, and interview. Your students will love this easy-to-use system.

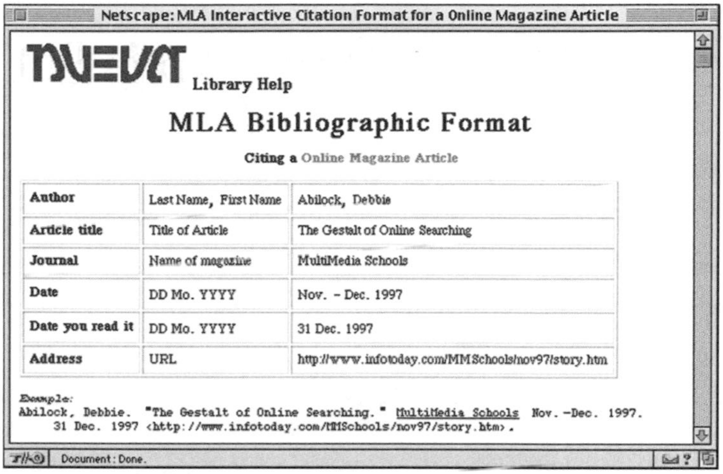

Netscape: MLA Interactive Citation Format for a Online Magazine Article

Library Help

MLA Bibliographic Format

Citing a Online Magazine Article

| | | |
|---|---|---|
| Author | Last Name, First Name | Abilock, Debbie |
| Article title | Title of Article | The Gestalt of Online Searching |
| Journal | Name of magazine | MultiMedia Schools |
| Date | DD Mo. YYYY | Nov. - Dec. 1997 |
| Date you read it | DD Mo. YYYY | 31 Dec. 1997 |
| Address | URL | http://www.infotoday.com/MMSchools/nov97/story.htm |

Example:
Abilock, Debbie. "The Gestalt of Online Searching." MultiMedia Schools Nov.-Dec. 1997. 31 Dec. 1997 <http://www.infotoday.com/MMSchools/nov97/story.htm>.

Document: Done.

**FIGURE 1.9 MLA Bibliographic Format**

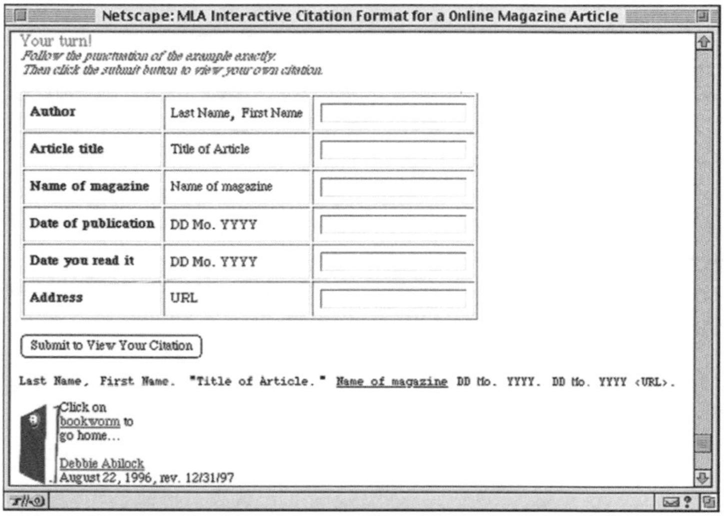

Netscape: MLA Interactive Citation Format for a Online Magazine Article

Your turn!
Follow the punctuation of the example exactly.
Then click the submit button to view your own citation.

| | | |
|---|---|---|
| Author | Last Name, First Name | |
| Article title | Title of Article | |
| Name of magazine | Name of magazine | |
| Date of publication | DD Mo. YYYY | |
| Date you read it | DD Mo. YYYY | |
| Address | URL | |

Submit to View Your Citation

Last Name, First Name. "Title of Article." Name of magazine DD Mo. YYYY. DD Mo. YYYY <URL>.

Click on bookworm to go home...

Debbie Abilock
August 22, 1996, rev. 12/31/97

**FIGURE 1.10 MLA Interactive Citation Formatter**

# CyberGuide Ratings

Karen McLachlan, Library Media Specialist at East Knox High School, Ohio, developed the rating guides (pages 20-21) to use with teachers and students. The WWW CyberGuides will help students explore and evaluate content when they are creating their own home pages.

# WWW CyberGuide Ratings for Content Evaluation

Title of site: _____
_____

Subject of site: _____
_____

URL (address): _____
_____

Considered for use with (class & grade level): _____
_____

Specific objective for using this site: _____
_____
_____
_____

Notes on possible uses of this site and URLs for individual site pages: _____
_____
_____
_____

Evaluate the Web site you are considering for instructional use according to the criteria described below. Circle the number which you feel the site deserves for each category: 5 = Excellent and 1 = Poor.

1. Speed
   - The home page downloads efficiently enough to use during whole-class instruction.                    5  4  3  2  1
   - The home page downloads efficiently enough to keep students on task during independent/small          5  4  3  2  1
     group study.

2. First impression/general appearance
   - The home page is designed attractively and will entice my students to further exploration.           5  4  3  2  1
   - The home page is designed clearly enough to be successfully manipulated by my intended users.         5  4  3  2  1

3. Ease of site navigation
   - My students will be able to move from page to page, link to link, item to item with ease and without  5  4  3  2  1
     getting lost or confused.
   - All links are clearly labeled and serve an easily identifiable purpose.                               5  4  3  2  1
   - Links provided to other pages and sites operate efficiently enough to keep my students on task.       5  4  3  2  1

## WWW CyberGuide Ratings for Content Evaluation *(cont.)*

4. Use of graphics/sounds/videos
   - The graphics/sounds/videos are clearly labeled, clearly identified.                     5 4 3 2 1
   - The graphics/sounds/videos serve a clear purpose appropriate for my intended audience.   5 4 3 2 1
   - The graphics/sounds/videos will aid my students in reaching the desired objectives for using this site.   5 4 3 2 1

5. Content/Information
   - This site offers a wealth of information related to my stated objectives.               5 4 3 2 1
   - The information is clearly labeled and organized, and will be easily understood by my students.   5 4 3 2 1
   - The content of linked sites is worthwhile and appropriate for my intended audience.      5 4 3 2 1
   - The content of linked sites adds to the value of this site for achieving my instructional goals.   5 4 3 2 1
   - The information providers are clearly identified.                                        5 4 3 2 1
   - The information providers are reliable.                                                  5 4 3 2 1
   - The content is free of bias, or the bias will be clearly recognized by my students.      5 4 3 2 1
   - This site provides interactivity which increases its instructional value.                5 4 3 2 1

6. The site was recently revised and is current.                                             5 4 3 2 1

7. Availability of further information
   - A contact person or address is readily available.                                       5 4 3 2 1

8. Add the total number of points you awarded to this site and determine your overall "WWW CyberGuide" rating. For any specific category that did not apply to this site, deduct five points from the total possible points.

   _____WWWWW (100-91 points). This site is so well designed and so effectively meets my instructional goals that I can provide my students with general instructions and allow free exploration.

   _____WWWW (90-76 points). This site contains good material but a site map with specific directions will assist my students in reaching the stated objectives.

   _____WWW (75-61 points). This site contains information that will make stops at designated points worthwhile, but students will need more structured guidance to reach my instructional goals. A list of bookmarks to specific pages and/or links is advisable, as is frequent discussion of student progress.

   _____WW (60-46 points). Although useful information exists at this site, its most effective contribution to my objectives will be in whole-class instruction where I can guide exploration and keep students on task.

   _____W (45-31 points). This site contains a few pieces of information that make it a possible alternative when other sources are not readily available. Supervised student use is advised.

## What Do You See?

On page 23 you'll find the photo analysis guide developed by the Library of Congress for the National Digital Institute held in Washington, D.C. The purpose of this guide is to assist teachers and students with visual literacy skills. The photograph used in this workshop was taken from one of the American Memory collections at the Library of Congress (http://memory.loc.gov), Touring Turn-of-the-Century America: Photographs from Detroit Publishing Company, 1880-1920 (http://lcweb2.loc.gov/ammen/detroit/dethome.html).

**FIGURE 1.12   For use with photo analysis guide: "Close of a Career in New York" http://lcweb2.loc.gov/ammem/detroit/dethome.html**

## What Do You See?

### Observation

Describe exactly what you see in the photo.

- What people and objects are shown?

- How are they arranged?

- What is the physical setting?

- What other details can you see?

### Knowledge

Summarize what you already know about the situation and time period shown, and the people and objects that appear.

### Interpretation

Say what you conclude from what you see.

- What's going on in the picture?

- Who are the people & what are they doing?

- What might be the function of the objects?

- What can we conclude about the time period?

### Further Research

What questions has the photo raised?
What are some sources I can use to find answers?

# Chapter 2

# Internet Resources

There are thousands of exit ramps to millions of pieces of information on the Internet. As an educator, parent, or student in K-12, you probably want to be able to explore the country roads and byways that will help you teach and learn. Road maps to these scenic areas will help you plan your journey down the information superhighway. These resources, project ideas, and lesson plans are not an exhaustive list, but will help you begin your adventure into the world of information access. The Internet is an evolving place. What you see today, may be gone tomorrow. Addresses and menu screens can change.

## GENERAL SITES

Several publications list new sites, contain articles about current topics, or share curriculum ideas. Some examples are shown here:

- IAT Infobits (http://www.iat.unc.edu/infobits/infobits.html). Infobits is an electronic service of the Institute for Academic Technology's Information Resources Group. Each month they monitor and select material from information and technology sources and provide brief annotations for electronic dissemination to educators. To subscribe to Infobits, send e-mail to listserv@unc.edu with the following message: SUBSCRIBE INFOBITS firstname lastname (substituting your own first and last names).

- Kathy Schrock's Guide for Educators (http://www.capecod.net/schrocguide/). Updated listing of Web sites of interest to educators. She also includes other useful tools such as Web evaluation guides.

- MultiMedia Schools magazine (http://www.infotoday.com/MMSchools). Three Internet columns from this leading print journal are posted on the Web with curriculum and how-to information. It is a great resource for teachers and library media professionals. "The Networks" covers the nuts and bolts of software and hardware, "Voices of Web" focuses on school-created and school-maintained home pages, and "CyberBee" takes an in-depth look at the best curriculum Web sites.

*MultiMedia Schools* (ISSN: 1075-0479) is published in print five times during the school year: September, November, January, March, and May. One-year subscriptions to *MultiMedia Schools* are available at the following rates for 1999: in the U.S.—$39.95; in Canada and Mexico—$54 (U.S.); outside North America—$63 (U.S.). For two-year and three-year discounts and for yearly rates beyond 1999, contact Information Today, Inc.'s customer service department, 800/300-9868 or custserv@infotoday.com. Mail check or purchase orders to:

Information Today, Inc.
143 Old Marlton Pike
Medford, NJ 08055-8750
Phone: 609-654-6266
Fax: 609-654-4309
E-mail: custserv@infotoday.com.

- Net-Happenings (http://scout.cs.wisc.edu/scout/net-hap/). Net-Happenings is a service of the Internet Scout Project in the Computer Sciences Department at the University of Wisconsin - Madison. It is produced and edited by Gleason Sackman, an Internet Scout Project staff member who works remotely from Fargo, North Dakota. The goal of Net-Happenings is to distribute announcements about Internet resources to network users and providers, and especially to the K-12 community. It is meant to be comprehensive, therefore postings number between forty and sixty per day, and are available via an e-mail distribution list in individual or digest (cumulative) format, or here at the Web site as soon as they are posted to the mailing list, with final postings being made by 3 PM CST/CDT, Monday through Friday. The postings are also available via a Usenet newsgroup, comp.internet.net-happenings.

• Online Educator (http://www.ole.net/ole/). A free weekly listing of education super sites is provided. By subscribing to the monthly journal, you will receive lesson ideas and ways to use computer technology in the classroom. Subscriptions are $34.95/year for the printed edition ($39.95 in Canada and $49.95 for overseas subscriptions) or $24.95/year for an e-mail version (check site for possible price changes). Mail checks or purchase orders to:

The Online Educator
3131 Turtle Creek Blvd., Suite 1250
Dallas, Texas 75219-5441
Phone: 800/672-6988
Fax orders to: 214/521-1021
E-mail: netsmart @dallas.net.

• Scout Report (http://scout.cs.wisc.edu/scout/report/). The Scout Report is the flagship publication of the Internet Scout Project. Published every Friday both on the Web and by e-mail, it provides a fast, convenient way to stay informed about valuable resources on the Internet. A team of professional librarians and subject matter experts select, research, and annotate each resource. To subscribe to the Scout Report, send an e-mail message to listserv@cs.wisc.edu with the following message: subscribe scout-report your first name your last name

# ART SITES

• Art Teacher Connection (http://www.primenet.com/~arted/). Here original lessons and ideas designed to incorporate computer technology into the visual arts are shared. The Digital Links Newsletter is available via e-mail for $25 a year.

- Artsedge (http://artsedge.kennedy-center.org). This is a good starting point for the arts. You will find lessons, links to museums, and ways to participate in community cultural events.

- ArtsEdNet—Starting Point (http://www.artsednet.getty.edu). Developed by the Getty Education Institute for the Arts, this Web site focuses on helping arts educators, general classroom teachers using the arts in their curriculum, museum educators, and university faculty involved in the arts. Discussions and articles encourage the exchange of ideas.

- ArtServe (https://rubens.anu.edu.au/index2.html). Australian National University's gallery of art history presents over 70,000 images of classical, medieval, and renaissance architecture and sculpture.

- Aunt Annie's Craft Page (http://www.auntannie.com). Grab your glue guns, scissors, and craft materials. Watch butterflies pop up from cards, geometric designs take shape, and animated stick puppets come to life. Complete illustrated step-by-step instructions, patterns, tie-in books, and links are provided. This is an exceptional Web site for elementary artists.

- Carlos's Coloring Book (http://coloring.com/). Choose between simple and expert modes. Pick from birthday, Christmas, crown, flower, house, or snowman pictures. Color them interactively and save them. This Web site is brought to you by Carlos A. Pero.

- Crayola Art Education (http://education.crayola.com/). Binny and Smith has produced an excellent resource for art teachers. There are directions for creating with many different types of art media. In addition, there is a history of crayons and contests that students can enter.

- French Ministry of Culture French Cave Paintings (http://www.culture. gouv.fr/culture/arcnat/chauvet/en/gvpda-d.htm). Text and images about the Chauvet Cave prehistoric cave art discovery are presented.

- Le Weblouvre (http://sunsite.unc.edu/louvre). Take a tour of the Louvre or Paris on this Web site. This is a wonderful resource for finding information about famous artists and viewing their work.

# CLIP ART SITES

• Animation Grove (http://www.dgill.simplenet.com/timagemap.html). You will find really cute animal cartoons here.

• Billy Bear's Bullets, Icons, & Clipart (http://www.billybear4kids.com/). Clearly, this is a winning place to go for all kinds of school-related clip art. Holiday images abound for decorating your newsletters and computer desktops.

• PageWorks—Kitty Roach (http://www.snowcrest.net/kitty/hpages/index. html). Lots of fun, whimsical characters can be found here along with information about how to animate your own icons.

• Icon Mania (http://www.kidsdomain.com/icon/index.html). Part of Kid's Domain, Icon Mania has a sampling of clip art collected from several different sites as well as original art. Specific instructions are provided on downloading and fair use.

• Kristy's Desktop Creations for Kids (http://www.kwebdesign.com/kdesk/). If you want cool and colorful animations, Kristy's Desktop Creations for Kids has tons of them. There are also screensavers and wallpaper.

# ECONOMICS SITES

• Economic Resources for K-12 Teachers (http://ecedweb.unomaha.edu/ teach.htm). Economics geared to K-12 is not an easy topic to find on the Web. This site provides lesson plans and other age-appropriate material. Don't miss the lesson titled "The Gang of 15" where students can solve a mystery using a currency converter program.

• Street Cents Online (http://www.halifax.cbc.ca/streetcents/). Consumer information for students is available at this site. It is based on the Canadian Broadcasting System's television show.

# ENCYCLOPEDIA SITES

Many of the encyclopedias on the Web feature articles from their publications and provide information on how to subscribe to their service.

- Britannica Online (http://www.eb.com). Free articles include women's history, D-Day, the Harlem Renaissance, and the British Invasion of the Beatles plus other musical groups. There are also links to educational sites that have been reviewed.

- Encarta (http://encarta.msn.com/). The concise Encarta is a free encyclopedia that retrieves a list of articles by keyword searching.

- Encyclopedia.Com (http://www.encyclopedia.com/). Encyclopedia.Com has over 17,000 short entries from the Concise Columbia Electronic Encyclopedia with premium services available from Electric Library for a fee.

- Grolier Interactive (http://gi.grolier.com/). The Presidency and a Commemorative of WWII are highlighted at this site. In addition is a Kid's Club area that has games and product information.

- Knowledge Adventure Encyclopedia (http://www.letsfindout.com/). Knowledge Adventure is a free kids encyclopedia with brief articles on hundreds of topics, some of which are illustrated. You can search by keyword or browse by subject.

- World Book Encyclopedia (http://www.worldbook.com/). Here you will find a neat interactive concentration game. First you match the pictures, then you find out detailed information about them. The pictures change from game to game. There are also selected articles from the World Book Encyclopedia.

# FOREIGN LANGUAGE SITES

- Foreign Languages for Travelers (http://www.travlang.com/languages). Elementary and middle school students will love looking up common words and phrases in different languages. About 60 percent of the words have audio files with pronunciations.

• National K-12 Foreign Language Resource Center—Starting Point (http://www.educ.iastate.edu/nflrc/homepage.htm). The National K-12 Foreign Language Resource Center at Iowa State University, Ames, Iowa, one of seven centers funded by the U.S. Department of Education, is committed to improving foreign language education in our nation's primary and secondary schools. Links to Web sites, professional development opportunities, and current news are provided at this site.

• Online Dictionaries and Translators (http://rivendel.com/~ric/resources/dictionary.html). An extensive list of links to all kinds of language dictionaries and translators will help students find the meaning of many obscure words.

# HEALTH AND NUTRITION SITES

• The Food Guide Pyramid (http://www.nal.usda.gov:8001/py/pmap.htm). This interactive site allows you to click on an item in the food pyramid and find out the daily dietary guidelines, what is included, and its preparation.

• Kids Food CyberClub (http://www.kidsfood.org/). Interactive games teach students about the importance of nutrition.

• HealthTouch Online (http://www.healthtouch.com/). This site provides information on diseases and prescription drugs.

• Colgate-Palmolive Kid's World (http://www.colgate.com/Kids-world/index.html). This Web site is for younger children who still believe in the tooth fairy. There are lots of fun activities.

• KidsHealth (http://kidshealth.org/). This contains health information geared to kids plus animations that help explain the body systems.

• Nutrition Cafe (http://www.exhibits.pacsci.org/nutrition/). This series of games is designed to help kids learn about nutrition.

# KEYPALS

- ePALS Classroom Exchange (http://www.epals.com/). Connect with classrooms from all over the world. It is also available in Spanish.

- Intercultural E-Mail Classroom Connections (http://www.stolaf.edu/network/iecc/). IECC is a free service designed to assist teachers in finding other classrooms to connect with for e-mail and projects.

# LANGUAGE ARTS SITES

- Alice's Adventures in Wonderland (http://www.megabrands.com/alice/goalice.html). Visit this site for a multimedia experience into Alice's Wonderland.

- Authors and Illustrators Who Visit Schools (http://www.teleport.com/~authilus/directory.htm). Authors and Illustrators Who Visit Schools is a directory service that lists fifteen authors and illustrators who will make a school visit. Useful information includes a photograph, awards, description of the program, fees, and how to contact the individual.

- Book Stacks Authors Pen (http://www.books.com/scripts/authors.exe). Browse the links to both contemporary and classical authors' Web sites. It is also a good place to find pictures of authors.

- BookRead (http://www.acs.ucalgary.ca/~dkbrown/bookread.txt). The Bookread project is designed to allow teachers and students to discuss the books they are reading with a partner classroom. To find others with whom to begin a BookRead partnership, subscribe to the BR_Match list:

  1. Send a message to: listproc@micronet.wcu.edu

  2. Subject: (blank)

  3. In the body, type: subscribe BR_Match firstname lastname (replace the names with your name or school name)

• Boys' Series Web Page (http://members.aol.com/biblioholc/bseries.html). This bibliographic list of the various boys' series includes Encyclopedia Brown and Brains Benton, among others. Biblioholics publishes a free, online newsletter about children's series called "Under the Attic Window." If you are interested in subscribing, send an e-mail message to: sharonr899@aol.com.

• Caldecott Award Page (http://www.ala.org/alsc/caldecott.html). This page covers art, reviews and lists of the Caldecott Award winners.

• Carol Hurst's Children's Literature Site (http://www.carolhurst.com/). Reviews of books, curriculum ideas, and professional resources are featured.

• Children's Book Council—Thirteen Exciting Reading Activities for Children (http://www.cbcbooks.org/navigation/teaindex.htm). These thirteen activities are designed to be starting points for hooking children on reading. They can be adapted for various grade levels. The ideas range from Reader's Theater, where students act out the books they have read, to drawing pictures. From these ideas you can begin to brainstorm your own.

• The Children's Literature Web Guide (http://www.acs.ucalgary.ca/~dkbrown/index.html). Here is a starting point for children's authors, illustrators, and publishers.

• Edward Lear (http://www2.pair.com/mgraz/Lear/index.html). Complete illustrated text of Lear's works is found here.

• English Teachers' Web Site (http://www.mlc.vic.edu.au/english/). Designed specifically for high school teachers, articles range from "Writing Introductory Paragraphs" to a guide on formatting your work based on computer technology.

• Girls' Series Web Page (http://members.aol.com/biblioholc/gseries.html). Bibliographic list of the various girls' series, including Nancy Drew and the Babysitters Club. There are lots of tie-in resources as well. Biblioholics publishes a free, online newsletter about a children's series called "Under the Attic Window." If you are interested in subscribing, send an e-mail message to: sharonr899@aol.com.

• The House of Usher: Edgar Allan Poe (http://www.comnet.ca/~forrest). Poetry, movie tie-ins, and sounds abound on this dramatic site.

• Internet Public Library (http://ipl.sils.umich.edu). A youth section has "Ask the Author" and how to say "hello" in over thirty languages.

• Invite an Author to Your School (http://www.snowcrest.net/kidpower/authors.html). Kid Power has gathered together a collection of links to authors who make school appearances. Teachers will be interested in reading the Frequently Asked Questions section. It provides information on how you invite an author to speak as well as helpful tips on making the visit successful.

• KidNews (http://www.kidnews.com/). KidNews is a free news and writing service for students and teachers around the world. Anyone may submit stories.

• KidzPage (http://web.aimnet.com/~veeceet/kids/kidzpage.html). This is a great tie-in to Ogden Nash poetry as well as a place for home grown verse.

• Newbery Award Page (http://www.ala.org/alsc/newbery.html). The page covers art, reviews, and lists of the Newbery Award winners.

• Read In (http://www.readin.org/). The Read In is a day-long reading project held once a year on the Internet. Students can chat with several contemporary authors. Register your school at the Web site and be sure to check out all of the activities to use with your students. Don't miss the promotional bookmarks featuring Webster B. Worm. You will need to download and install the free chat program, Palace. It runs on either Macintosh or Windows. In addition, there are also special events throughout the year. Check the Web site for details.

• The SCOOP Adventure Page (http://www.friend.ly.net/scoop/adventure). Interactive stories with different story lines let students choose what will happen next.

• Seussville (http://www.randomhouse.com/seussville/). There are lots of activities and games, plus the story of Dr. Suess.

• Theodore Tugboat (http://www.cochran.com/theodore/). Choose your own adventure with Theodore Tugboat, download a page from the online coloring book, or share ideas via e-mail.

• Vandergrift's Children's Literature Page (http://www.scils.rutgers.edu/special/kay/childlit.html). Many thoughtful ideas on children's literature as well as book lists that she uses in her university classes are offered here. There are beautiful illustrations, too!

# MATH SITES

• Aunty Math (http://www.dcmrats.org/AuntyMath.html). Math challenges for kids.

• BasketMath Online (http://www.scienceacademy.com/BI/index.html). BasketMath will provide drills and practice from addition to verbal reasoning.

• Blue Dog Can Count (http://www.forbesfield.com/bdf.html). An interactive program starring Blue Dog allows students to input math problems and hear Blue Dog bark out the answers.

• Cuisenaire Kid's Page (http://www.cuisenaire-dsp.com/start_kids.html). Let Albert the Inchworm lead your K-2 students through measuring activities at the Cuisenaire Learning Page.

• Elementary Problem of the Week (http://forum.swarthmore.edu/elempow/). Math problem is geared to Grades 3-6.

- Geometry Problem of the Week (http://forum.swarthmore.edu/geopow/index.html). A problem is posted each week during the school year. Students can submit solutions.

- Graphing Calculator Main Page (http://oit.iusb.edu/~spowell/graph.html). Today a graphing calculator is one of the most important tools in a teenager's backpack. So, which model do you choose? Where can you find programs? How do you connect it to a computer? Sam Powell, a high school mathematics/computer teacher has created the Graphing Calculator Main Page to answer these questions and more.

- Home Team—Math, Baseball & The San Francisco Giants! (http://www.kn.pacbell.com/wired/baseball/). This is a clever search and find game using math and Web sites to determine the cost of attending a San Francisco Giants Baseball game.

- Houghton Mifflin Math Central (http://www.eduplace.com/math/mathcentral/index.html). Brain Teasers for all grade levels are posted weekly.

- Interactive Mathematics Miscellany and Puzzles (http://www.cut-the-knot.com/). Using Java applets, Interactive Mathematics Miscellany and Puzzles, this site puts theory into practice. All sorts of mathematical questions are explored beginning with a hypothesis or premise followed by an actual problem or model to solve.

- Investing for Kids (http://library.advanced.org/3096/). Create and track stock portfolios, then compare their performance over a period of time.

- Internet Pizza Server (http://www.ecst.csuchico.edu/~pizza/). Cook up virtual pizza from the Internet Pizza Server. Ordinary as well as tongue-in-cheek toppings can be chosen.

- Internet Pizza Server—Lesson (http://www.cs.rice.edu/~sboone/Lessons/Titles/pizza.html). Begin your virtual feast with Susan Boone's lesson.

- Kid Klok (http://mambo.ucsc.edu/psl/kk.html). This is an interactive online clock. Kids can experiment with telling time.

- Math and Science Pavilion—Graphing Calculators (http://pen.k12.va.us/ Anthology/Pav/MathSci/calc/Calc.html). A great place for CASIO programs is the Math and Science Pavilion of Virginia Public Education Network. Who can resist experimenting with program titles like "In the Kitchen with Mama Mia: Max-Min Applications," "Barnum & Bailey Meet the Graphing Calculator," or "Javelins and Pirates: Using Parametric Equations to Model Projectile Motion"?

- Math Baseball (http://www.gold-pages.com/math/). Math Baseball, another interactive program, focuses on addition and multiplication at three different levels of difficulty.

- Math Forum (http://forum.swarthmore.edu/). Browse or search this gold mine of links to math Web pages. Dig through Steve's Dump for a variety of curriculum links divided into various subject categories. Also home to Ask Dr. Math and Elementary Problem of the Week.

- Mathmania (http://csr.uvic.ca/~mmania/). Activities abound, including research, experiments on knots, sorting networks, finite-state machines, and graphs.

- MEGA Math (http://www.c3.lanl.gov/mega-math/index.html). Open-ended math problems stimulate critical thinking.

- Mr. E's Home Page—Algebra (http://www.visi.com/~dethier/). These are hands-on strategies for helping students with algebra problems.

- National Council of Teachers of Mathematics (NCTM) (http://www. nctm.org/). Ideas for the classroom and discussions on standards are some of the many topics covered.

- Public Schools of North Carolina (http://www.dpi.state.nc.us/Curriculum/ CrrclmMtrx.html). The North Carolina Department of Public Instruction has constructed a matrix listing its entire K-12 curriculum competency goals.

- Pythagoras' Playground (http://www.kyes-world.com/pythagor.htm). Make a Quadrant and learn how to use it for measuring. There are fun activities for investigating triangles.

- Shack's Page of Math Problems (http://www.thewizardofodds.com/math/). It contains math problems to solve with a degree-of-difficulty rating. Many are logic problems.

- Web Mind (http://einstein.et.tudelft.nl/~mvdlaan/WebMind/WM_intro.html). This is an interactive game similar to MasterMind.

- ticalc.org (http://www.ticalc.org/). ticalc.org is a page devoted to programs for Texas Instruments calculators. News and frequently asked questions are a few of the many items available.

# MUSIC SITES

- BMG Classic World Composers (http://www.classicalmus.com/bmg-cgi-bin/ dbm/composers). Browse or search for biographical information and album titles of classical composers in the various music periods in history.

- Internet Resources for Music Teachers—Starting Point (http://www. isd77.k12.mn.us/resources/staffpages/shirk/music.html). Cynthia Shirk, a music teacher, has compiled a list of links that are useful to teachers. A special feature on the page is the Music Box of Sound and Software, with complete downloadable music compositions in QuickTime format.

- Looney Tunes Karaoke (http://www.kids.warnerbros.com/karaoke). Sing along with the Looney Tunes gang at this Web site.

• Sony Artist Information (http://www.music.sony.com/Music/ArtistInfo/index.html). Information about artists under the Sony label is presented.

# PHYSICAL EDUCATION SITES

• Games Kids Play (http://www.corpcomm.net/~gnieboer/gamehome.htm). Investigate the rules and directions for playing games from marbles to red-light green-light.

• PE Central (http://pe.central.vt.edu). Many activities are provided for PE teachers to use in their curriculum, including interdisciplinary lessons. It is also the best place for physical education teachers to find current information about the American Master Teacher Program, an in-service workshop designed to help teachers learn about the latest teaching methods in physical education.

# SCIENCE SITES

• Access Excellence (http://www.gene.com/ae). Don't miss this site. It is by far one of the richest sources of biology and biotechnology material on the Web. You can actively discuss a variety of subjects through online seminars, join a teacher's discussion group, read the latest news about science discoveries, or browse the hundreds of classroom activities written by teachers.

• American Museum of Natural History (http://www.amnh.org/Exhibition/index.html). Who are the people behind the bones? What contributions did they make to paleontology? "Personalities in Paleontology" showcases ten leading individuals complete with pictures and short biographies. Ever wonder what the environment would look like during geologic history? An artist's depiction in the Timelines section lets you imagine a scene from a specific period and explains the habitat. How should T-Rex be mounted for display? To find the current theory, click on six new halls. Vertebrate evolution is illustrated with numerous drawings.

• Athena (http://athena.wednet.edu/). Earth and space science lessons are showcased for grades K-12.

• Aurora Page (http://www.geo.mtu.edu/weather/aurora/). Information and images are posted about the Northern Lights.

• B-Eye (http://cvs.anu.edu.au/andy/beye/beyehome.html). See the world through the eye of a bee.

• Bill Beaty's Amateur Science (http://www.eskimo.com/~billb/amasci.html). With its list of links to lots of hobbies and science topics, it's a great place to look for hands-on activities.

• Bill Nye the Science Guy (http://nyelabs.kcts.org). Based on the popular PBS television show, and like Mr. Wizard a generation ago, this upbeat Web site is designed to interest children in the world of science. Discover fast facts and experiments from the pull-down menus in the U-NYE-Verse episode guide.

• Boyce Thompson Southwestern Arboretum (http://ag.arizona.edu/BTA/). This contains a very nice explanation of desert plants.

• BugWatch (http://bugwatch.com/bugindex.html). Check out this source for insect information.

• Cells Alive (http://www.cellsalive.com). Cool animations of how cells work.

• Cornell Theory Center Math and Science Gateway (http://www.tc.cornell.edu/Edu/MathSciGateway/math.html). Teachers and secondary students in grades 9-12 will appreciate this site designed to meet their needs. It was compiled so students would have an easier time finding information about astronomy, biology, chemistry, computing, the environment, health, mathematics, and physics. Each reference includes a brief annotation.

• Dinosaur Trace Fossils (http://www.emory.edu/GEOSCIENCE/HTML/ Dinotraces.htm). In our zeal to focus on the dinosaurs themselves, we often overlook the area of trace fossils. These are tracks, trails, burrows, borings, gnawings, eggs, nests, gizzard stones, and dung. An excellent place to learn more about this subject is at Emory University's Trace Fossils site.

• Dinosauria—University of California at Berkeley (http://www.ucmp. berkeley.edu/diapsids/dinosaur.html). One of the best places to start for finding general information about dinosaurs. Learn all about current research in Dinosbuzz, a newsletter that gives a thorough explanation of the theories on extinction, dinosaurs' possible evolutionary relationship to birds, and the differences between fact and fiction of dinosaurs portrayed in the movies. To better understand the groups of dinosaurs, read Dinosaur Diversity and Dispelling Myths. Join Sam Welles, professor emeritus, on a narrated tour of his discovery of Dilophosaurus beginning in the summer of 1942. Find out why the name changed after several years of investigation and how he viewed Dilophosaurus as a movie star in Jurassic Park. The site is searchable, has a glossary of terms, and links to the geologic time machine.

• Eisenhower National Clearinghouse (http://www.enc.org). Here you will find a comprehensive resource for science and math materials, how much they cost, and where to purchase them. In addition, there are links to lessons plus the Digital Dozen, monthly picks of the best Web sites.

• Elementary Science Program (http://www.monroe2boces.org/shared/esp/). Science units teach with Web links.

• Endangered Species (http://www.nceet.snre.umich.edu/EndSpp/Endangered. html). This is one of the best sites for facts on endangered species.

• Explorer—Lesson Plans & Curriculum (http://explorer.scrtec.org/ explorer/). Many of the math and science lessons can be used to teach scientific methods of observation and analysis. Particularly beneficial are the activities on statistics and probability in the mathematics folder.

Each activity was written by an educator and is labeled with the appropriate grade level.

• Fall Colors in Missouri (http://www.conservation.state.mo.us/nathis/seasons/fall/fall.html). Here is the answer to why leaves change color.

• Five Senses (http://www.sedl.org/scimath/pasopartners/senses/welcome.html). It contains a detailed lesson plan.

• Frog Dissection (http://curry.edschool.Virginia.EDU/go/frog/menu.html). Online tutorial teaches high school students how to dissect a frog.

• Froggy Page (http://frog.simplenet.com/froggy/). This fun page on frogs has sounds, pictures, and information.

• The Heart: An Online Exploration—Franklin Institute of Science (http://sln.fi.edu/biosci/heart.html). A virtual exploration of the heart is given.

• Inquiry Almanack (http://sln.fi.edu/qa97). It contains a monthly almanac of interesting science facts and activities from the Franklin Institute of Science.

• Interactive Knee (http://www.rad.upenn.edu/rundle/InteractiveKnee.html). The University of Pennsylvania Medical Center provides different views of the knee with explanations.

• Invention Dimension (http://web.mit.edu/invent). An Inventor of the Week is profiled.

• Microworlds: Exploring the Structure of Material (Grades 9-12) (http://www.lbl.gov/MicroWorlds/). MicroWorlds is an interactive tour of current research in the materials sciences at Berkeley Lab's Advanced Light Source.

• Missouri Botanical Gardens (http://www.mobot.org/MBGnet/index2.htm). The MBGNet is an excellent starting point if you are studying biomes in your elementary science classroom. It covers the rain forest to the tundra to the desert with lots of facts and illustrations.

• NASA SpaceLink (http://spacelink.nasa.gov). Spacelink is an educational resource on aeronautics and space.

• National Science Teachers Association (http://www.nsta.org).Organization news and standards for science teachers are presented.

• Neuroscience for Kids (http://weber.u.washington.edu/~chudler/neurok. html). Lots of graphics and animations that explain the nervous system make this a fascinating site for students.

• Northern Lights Planetarium (http://www.uit.no/npt/homepage-npt.en. html). This is an exhibit from Norway with information about Aurora Borealis from both a scientific and human perspective.

• Odyssey of the Mind (http://www.odyssey.org/odyssey). This organization sponsors team-based problem solving activities for students. Included is information on how to join.

• Optics for Kids (http://www.opticalres.com/kidoptx.html). Illustrated article shows how lenses work.

• Paper Dinosaurs 1824–1969 (http://www.lhl.lib.mo.us/pubserv/hos/dino/ welcome.htm). Highlighting this extraordinary exhibit is original source material from the collections of the Linda Hall Library, Kansas City, Missouri. The curators have gathered over eighty printed works about dinosaur discoveries and lore—such as why one scientist called T-Rex "Teddysaurus." You will learn about the pioneers, read their findings, and view over 136 impressive dinosaur drawings and images.

• Prem's Fossil Gallery or Beneath the Calamites Tree (http://www.noblestar. net/~prem/fossil.html). All of your aspiring rock hounds will want to read the Fossil Hunting FAQ at Prem's Fossil Gallery. This amateur collector has assembled a topnotch display of trilobites, graphtolites, and fossil plants. Another good source for tips is the Fossil Hunter. Information on collecting locations, a field trip checklist, rules, and safety is supplied.

- Royal Tyrrell Museum (http://tyrrell.magtech.ab.ca). Want to dig for fossils or save the dinosaurs? The Explorers Program will direct you to current information on trips that range from day digs to lengthier field experiences. World renowned paleontologists lead you on fascinating journeys throughout North America.

- Science Learning Network (http://www.sln.org). This is a good starting point for science activities in the classroom. The Science Learning Network is made up of a consortium of museums.

- Sea World Busch Gardens (http://www.seaworld.org/). It contains an animal information database.

- Smithsonian (http://www.si.edu/). This is a gateway to many of the servers from the Smithsonian, including the National Air & Space Museum, Natural History Web, and the Photo Server of images from the museum collections.

- Space Calendar (http://www.jpl.nasa.gov/calendar/). Included are space-related activities and anniversaries for the coming year. Launch dates are subject to change. Anniversary dates are listed in five-year increments. There are links to pictures and text about the events.

- StemNet Science Fair Home Page (http://www.stemnet.nf.ca/~jbarron/scifair.html). Comprehensive information is given about science fairs and project ideas by grade levels.

- The T.W.I.N.K.I.E.S. Project (http://www.owlnet.rice.edu/~gouge/twinkies.html). Not even the most reluctant learner can ignore this cleverly constructed Web page. Tongue-in-cheek humor is used to describe procedures, observations, and possible applications when experimenting with cream-stuffed sponge cakes. Nuke them in a microwave to find out just how resistant they are to radiation. Dunk them in water to see their solubility. Blend them to see how much air they contain.

- Virology (http://www.bocklabs.wisc.edu/Welcome.html). View pictures of microscopic viruses and learn information about them.

- Virtual Fly Lab (http://vflylab.calstatela.edu). Choose characteristics from visual choices displayed on the page for a male and female fruit fly, then mate them. The resulting fruit fly will be displayed on the screen with details about its characteristics. This is a great program for the study of genetics. And you thought all fruit flies looked alike!

- Volcano World (http://volcano.und.edu). Current and historical information about volcanoes is given in addition to numerous photographs.

- Welcome to the Planets (http://pds.jpl.nasa.gov/planets/). Welcome to the Planets contains planet profiles, pictures, and descriptions of the space vehicles that were used in their exploration. This is a good resource for students interested in this topic.

- Why Files (http://whyfiles.news.wisc.edu). Every two weeks a new article is posted that focuses on current science topics in the news. You can use these with students to generate discussions in the classroom. The files are archived.

- You Can with Beakman and Jax (http://www.youcan.com). Zany site presents fifty questions on topics kids will love. One example is, "Why do feet smell?"

- Yuckiest Site on the Internet (http://www.yucky.com). One of the top sites on the Internet, it has tons of activities dealing with worms, cockroaches, and the body.

# SOCIAL STUDIES SITES

## African Americans

- Afro-American Myths and Fables (http://www.afroam.org/children/myths/myths.html). "Why Crocodile Has a Rough Back" and "The Lion and the Hare" are two examples from a marvelous collection of myths and fables. Each story begins with a statement on its origin. Elementary children will love viewing the illustrations while reading the stories.

- Awale: The Art of African Game (http://www.myriad-online.com/awale. htm). Oware (pronounced oh-wah-ruh) is a game that has its origins in Ethiopia. There are a number of variations including Awale and Wari. The game is played with a hollow wood plank and some stones or seeds. Because it is a strategy game, you may want to tie it into problem-solving lessons. Awale, an elegant shareware program, is designed for both Macintosh and Windows. A trial copy can be downloaded for review.

- Faces of Science: African Americans in Science (http://www.lib.lsu.edu/ lib/chem/display/faces.html). Information on the lives of scientists.

- The Harlem Renaissance—Encarta Schoolhouse (http://encarta.com/ schoolhouse/harlem/harlem.asp). Brief information about the period with a few links to some of the people like Billie Holiday and W.E.B. DuBois.

- A Journey Through Art with W. H. Johnson (http://nmaa-ryder.si.edu/ johnson/intro3.html). William Johnson (1901-1970), a major figure in 20th-century American Art, studied at the National Academy of Design in New York. Prior to World War II he spent time learning from European artists in southern France. You are invited to journey through a chronological timeline of Johnson's works. In this series of colorful paintings, you can observe how his style evolved. The "Fighters for Freedom" collection depicts famous men and women who were leaders in the quest for racial equality. In "Scenes from City Life and Country Life," universal themes are portrayed that touch the human spirit. Activities for elementary students, such as creating a self-portrait, planning a make-believe trip, or writing a story about one of the paintings, accompany each page.

- Martin Luther King, Jr. (http://www.seattletimes.com/mlk/index.html). *Seattle Times* article commemorates the 30th anniversary of his death.

- Martin Luther King, Jr. Tribute (http://www.pathfinder.com/Life/mlk/mlk. html). Pictures from *Life* magazine appear here.

- Photo Site Presents Influential African Americans of the 20th Century (http://www.pathfinder.com/photo/essay/african/home.htm). This site is a photo essay of African Americans.

- Stamp on Black History (http://library.advanced.org/10320). Beginning in 1940, African Americans were recognized on U.S. postage stamps for their contributions and achievements in a variety of areas. This beautiful collection contains a picture of each stamp and information about the featured individual. There are word searches, puzzles, coloring pages, recipes, writing, and math activities that tie-in to the curriculum. Spark the interest of your reluctant students by visiting this fun site.

- The Underground Railroad (http://www.nationalgeographic.com/features /99/railroad/j1.html). Take a journey on the underground railroad on this interactive Web site. Learn about the routes, the hardships, and the miles that had to be traveled to reach freedom. Classroom ideas are provided for all grade levels.

# Biography

- Abraham Lincoln Online (http://www.netins.net/showcase/creative/lincoln. html). It presents an extensive list of links from historic places to speeches.

- Anne Frank Online (http://www.annefrank.com/). This site is brought to us by the Anne Frank Center USA, which also sponsors a traveling exhibit and the Spirit of Anne Frank Awards. Most will be visiting this page for information about Anne Frank and the photographs that accompany Her Life and Times. The publishing history of her diary with excerpts is a wonderful tribute to her memory and to the ordeal of the millions who perished in the Holocaust.

- Biography (http://www.biography.com). Over 20,000 short biographies are presented, plus videoclips and programming.

- Mr. Showbiz Celeb Site (http://celebsite.com). Biographies of movie stars, TV personalities, and sports stars are contained here.

# Civil War

- •American Civil War Home Page—Starting Point (http://sunsite.utk.edu/civil-war/). This is one of the most comprehensive lists of links to Civil War related material.

- • Artifacts of Assassination—American Treasures of the Library of Congress (http://www.loc.gov/exhibits/treasures/trm012.html). This exhibit from the Library of Congress shows the contents of Lincoln's pockets at the time of his assassination.

- • Civil War Maps—American Treasures of the Library of Congress (http://www.loc.gov/exhibits/treasures/trm010.html). These maps are three examples from Jedediah Hotchkiss (1828–1899), a topographic engineer found in the Confederate States Army who prepared maps and provided geographic intelligence for Thomas J. "Stonewall" Jackson, Robert E. Lee, Richard Ewell, Jubal Early, and John B. Gordon.

- • Civil War Women (http://scriptorium.lib.duke.edu/collections/civil-war-women.html). Original source material from Duke University about women and their role in the Civil War, including diaries and photographs.

- • Custer's Civil War Command—American Treasures of the Library of Congress (http://www.loc.gov/exhibits/treasures/trm011.html). These treasures are from the prints and manuscript division of the Library of Congress.

- • Gettysburg Address (http://lcweb.loc.gov/exhibits/gadd/). This exhibit from the Library of Congress has drafts of the Gettysburg Address, translated into twenty-eight languages, and the only known photograph of Lincoln at Gettysburg.

- • Letters from an Iowa Soldier in the Civil War (http://www.ucsc.edu/civil-war-letters/home.html). This is a collection of letters written by Newton Robert Scott to Hannah Cone about his personal experiences during the Civil War.

• Moses Horton (http://www.unc.edu/lib/mssinv/exhibits/horton/). George Moses Horton (ca. 1797–ca.1883) was a Chatham County, North Carolina, slave who taught himself to read and compose poetry. By the age of twenty, he began visiting the University of North Carolina and selling the students acrostic love poems based on the names of their girlfriends. His literary efforts were encouraged by a number of well-placed individuals, including the novelist Caroline Lee Hentz, North Carolina Governor and later University President David L. Swain, and newspaperman Horace Greeley.

• Poetry and Music of the War Between the States (http://www.erols.com/kfraser/). Midi files are used to deliver musical renditions of Civil War tunes.

• Selected Civil War Photographs—American Memory Collection (http://lcweb2.loc.gov/ammem/cwphome.html). Mathew Brady photographs portray battlefields and people.

## Geography

• 50 States of the United States (http://www.50states.com/). Brief information is given about each state.

• Color Landform Atlas of the United States (http://fermi.jhuapl.edu/states/states.html). The Color Landform Atlas of the United States supplies a topographic and county outline map for each state except Alaska and Hawaii.

• GeoNet Game (http://www.hmco.com/hmco/school/geo/). GeoNet is an interactive online game with varying degrees of difficulty. You answer a series of questions based on geography in order to save the planet.

• Finding Your Way with Map and Compass (http://www.usgs.gov/factsheets/finding-your-way/finding-your-way.html). U.S. Geological Survey explains how to use a map and compass together to get from one point to another.

- How to Use a Compass (http://www.uio.no/~kjetikj/compass/). Illustrated instructions take you through three lessons starting with the rudiments of directions, then move on to compass and map interaction to more complex magnetic map declination.

- Map Machine—National Geographic (http://www.nationalgeographic.com/resources/ngo/maps/). Interactive map helps to locate geographical areas.

- MapBlast (http://www.mapblast.com). Create your own map by typing in an address.

- Mapmaker, Mapmaker, Make Me a Map (http://loki.ur.utk.edu/ut2kids/maps/map.html). This is a nice discussion on how cartographers make maps.

- MapQuest (http://www.mapquest.com/). Create your own travel map with MapQuest.

- Perry-Castañeda Library Map Collection (http://www.lib.utexas.edu/Libs/PCL/Map_collection/Map_collection.html). Hundreds of maps are available from the University of Texas at Austin, which houses the Perry-Castañeda Library (PCL) collection, a good source for contemporary and historical material. Since the PCL maps have no copyright, they can be downloaded and used for any purpose.

# Government

- The American Presidency—Grolier Online (http://gi.grolier.com/presidents/preshome.html). Articles are given about each of the presidents.

- Office of the Clerk, On-line Legislative Resource Center, U.S. House (http://clerkweb.house.gov/). At this site, you can obtain copies of bills and House documents, find historical information about the House of Representatives, and learn how to review documents the Clerk makes available as part of the public disclosure responsibilities.

• Hall of Presidents (http://www.npg.si.edu/col/pres/index.htm). Explore the National Portrait Gallery of paintings and information about the Presidents.

• National Park Service (http://www.nps.gov). Parknet is a comprehensive directory of the National Park Service. For each park, information includes address, telephone number, hours of operation, directions, entrance fees, facilities, and more. "Ask a Ranger," "This Day in Park History," "Naturenet," and "Links to the Past" are a few of the other features you will want to use in your classroom.

• Portraits of Presidents and First Ladies 1789-Present (http://memory.loc. gov/ammem/odmdhtml/preshome.html). Images of all the presidents and most of the first ladies are chronicled here.

• President (http://sunsite.unc.edu/lia/president/pres-home.html). This site provides links to Presidential Library Web sites.

• Presidential Inaugural—Smithsonian (http://photo2.si.edu/inaugural/inau_top/ inaugural.html). Look over documentary photographs of inaugural events.

• THOMAS Legislative Online (http://thomas.loc.gov/). Follow the legislative process of current bills in Congress, learn about how a bill becomes a law, or find information about government.

• U. S. Historical Documents (http://www.law.ou.edu/ushist.html). A very nice exhibit of state flags can be found at the University of Oklahoma along with a superb chronology of American historical documents.

• U.S. House of Representatives (http://www.house.gov/). Tour the U.S. House of Representatives and find information about current members.

• United Nations (http://www.un.org/). Review this information about the United Nations and its programs.

• United States Senate (http://www.senate.gov/). Tour the U.S. Senate and find information about current members.

- Vote Smart (http://www.vote-smart.org/). This Web site tracks the records of politicians and provides useful election information.

- Web Central—Government Information (http://www.cio.com/central/government.html). A list of links to government pages worldwide is presented.

- The White House (http://www.whitehouse.gov/). On the White House Web server, you can listen to messages from the President and Vice-President, learn about the First Family, ask questions, and send e-mail.

# Immigration

- Ellis Island (http://www.i-channel.com/features/ellis/). Look back at immigration through the voices and histories of immigrants.

- New York, NY, Ellis Island—Immigration: 1900–1920 (http://cmp1.ucr.edu/exhibitions/immigration_id.html). Twenty-four images from the Keystone-Mast Collection, California Museum of Photography, give a view of Ellis Island during the height of immigration.

- Tenement Museum—New York at the turn of the century (http://www.wnet.org/tenement/). Personal perspectives on the Tenement as history and housing are presented.

# Law

- Teens Court TV (http://www.courttv.com/teens/). Teens Court TV is designed to give teenagers an inside look at the justice system. Surveys, a legal dictionary, and interactive features are available.

# History

- American Memory (http://lcweb2.loc.gov/ammem/). In words, pictures, and sounds, the American Memory Collection offers us the unique opportunity to dig through original source material and bring living history into our classrooms.

• Betsy Ross Home Page (http://www.libertynet.org/iha/betsy/index.html). Questions about the American flag can be directed to the Betsy Ross site. It includes her story, famous quotes, facts, timeline, picture gallery of the flag in history, etiquette, trivia, and links to other places.

• Byzantine & Medieval Studies Sites—Starting Point (http://www.fordham. edu/halsall/medweb/). This extensive list of links to the ancient world includes annotations of some sites.

• Cybrary of the Holocaust (http://remember.org/). There are many resources about the Holocaust, including journals of survivors, historical perspectives, and witness facts.

• Historic Paper Dolls (http://www.ushsdolls.com/). Colorful costumes adorn these classic paper dolls.

• Historic Valley Forge (http://libertynet.org/iha/valleyforge/). The story of Valley Forge is presented along with other interesting information.

• History Place (http://www.historyplace.com/). Lots of photographs and chronological data support varying themes from American and World History.

• History/Social Studies Web Site for K-12 Teachers—Starting Point (http://www.execpc.com/~dboals/boals.html). This is one of the best annotated lists of links to history and social studies Web sites on the Net. Start here before you search.

• The Labyrinth: Resources for Medieval Studies (http://www.georgetown. edu/labyrinth/). The Labyrinth Project from Georgetown University links databases, text, and images on Medieval Studies, including French, Iberian, Italian, Latin, Middle English, and Old English. Subjects cover Anglo-Saxon, Byzantium, Celtic, England (1066-1500), France, Germany, Iberia, Italy, and Scandinavian Cultures.

- Old Timer's Page (http://www.lis.ab.ca/walton/old/default.htm). The Old Timer's Place is a source for information about how things used to be made. It includes information on soap making, butter churns, and making a cistern.

- Seven Wonders of the Ancient World (http://pharos.bu.edu/Egypt/Wonders/). This is an excellent page offering a scholarly look at the history, descriptions, and pictures of the Seven Wonders of the Ancient World. Only one of these ancient wonders exists today.

- United States Holocaust Memorial Museum (http://www.ushmm.org/). Several features are included at this online exhibit of information about the Holocaust. The Hidden History of the Kovno Ghetto shows how a people clandestinely documented their history as a legacy to generations to come. The Spirit of St. Louis tells the sad story of a group of Jewish refugees on a ship that no country would accept. Now, stories are being gathered from the survivors and their descendents. In addition to the online exhibits, there is information about visiting the museum.

## Multicultural

- AskAsia (http://www.askasia.org/). Sponsored by the Asia Society, the site has a wealth of lesson plans.

- K-5 CyberTrail Multicultural Curriculum Resources (http://www.wmht.org/trail/explor02.htm). Read over this annotated list of resources for multicultural education.

- Multicultural Pavilion—Starting Point (http://curry.edschool.virginia.edu/go/multicultural/). Teacher resources, international projects, and research are only a few of the many links available.

## Native Americans

- Encyclopedia Mythica—Native American Mythology (http://www.pantheon.org/mythica/areas/native_american/). The legend of the Buffalo

Dance is one of the many stories you can locate at the Web site. Browse through the various tribal names for more stories.

• First Nations Histories (http://dickshovel.com/Compacts.html). Brief histories about Native American tribes.

• History of Tecumseh and Tippecanoe (http://www.tippecanoe.com/tec_hist.htm). Read about the History of Tecumseh and the battle at Tippecanoe Creek.

• National Portrait Gallery: Native Americans (http://www.npg.si.edu/col/native/). Portraits and descriptions are given of thirteen Native Americans.

• Native American Foods (http://indy4.fdl.cc.mn.us/~isk/food/recipes.html). Recipes for frybread, tacos, pumpkin, and much more can be located at this Web site.

# Westward Expansion

• Across the Plains in 1844 (http://www3.pbs.org/weta/thewest/wpages/wpgs620/sager1.htm). Catherine Sager Pringle wrote her diary in 1860 about the journey from Missouri to Oregon. She originally emigrated from Ohio with her family to Missouri. She relates incidents on the trail, the poignant story of her father's and mother's deaths, and her days in Indian captivity.

• Advice from William Todd—1846 (http://calcite.rocky.edu/octa/todd.htm). William Todd writes home about the tribulations of ascending mountains by literally "throwing their wagons like handspikes." His reports were published in the Sangamo Journal (Springfield, Illinois).

• Bison Company (http://www.buffalostampede.com/). Find everything you ever wanted (or didn't want) to know about eating buffalo, including nutritional information, its history as a food item, and recipes.

- Buffalo Soldiers of the Western Frontier (http://www.imh.org/imh/buf/buftoc.html). The International Horse Museum presents the history of the Buffalo Soldiers beginning in 1866.

- California As I Saw It: First Person Narratives of California's Early Years, 1849–1900 (http://lcweb2.loc.gov/ammem/cbhtml/cbhome.html). Read eyewitness accounts during California's development.

- California Gold Country Highway 49 Revisited (http://www.malakoff.com./gcframe.htm). Travel along Highway 49 and learn about the gold-mining camps of yesteryear.

- Chuck Wagon Cooking (http://www.netarrant.net/interact/events/cookbook/cwcook.htm). This online booklet written by Jalyn Burkett, Tarrant County Extension Director in Texas, provides an interesting introduction into the history of chuck wagon cooking along with recipes.

- Commerce of the Prairies—Josiah Gregg (http://www.ukans.edu/carrie/kancoll/books/gregg/contents.htm). First published in 1844, this two-volume book contains the travel stories of Josiah Gregg, a Santa Fe trader. Chapters cover the origin and development of the Santa Fe trade route, the harnessing of pack mules, and preparations for trips.

- Diary of Emily Towell—1881 (http://www.cybernet1.com/homestyle/emily.htm). Emily Towell writes a fascinating day-by-day account of the daily occurrences of trail life, from the sad departure of loved ones, to the excitement of a rabbit barbecue, and to the unexpected treat of mountain trout.

- Donner Online (http://www.kn.pacbell.com/wired/donner/). Learn about the tragic events surrounding the ill-fated Donner Party using this Web-based lesson developed by Education First, Pacific Bell Knowledge Network. Students assume the roles of historian, cartographer, diarist, correspondent, jester, provisioner, or scientist and complete a series of activities using a series of hyperlinked sites. A Hyperstudio template for publishing student projects complements the lesson and can be downloaded from the site.

• Images of the American West (http://www.treasurenet.com/images/ameri canwest/). This site features selected images from the National Archives.

• In Search of the Oregon Trail (http://www.pbs.org/opb/oregontrail/ or http://www.isu.edu/~trinmich/Oregontrail.html). In Search of the Oregon Trail examines the myth and exposes the truth behind America's journey west. An extensive online teacher's guide includes a time line, classroom activities, printable map, curriculum standards, and resources.

• Letters and Journals of Narcissa Whitman 1836–1847 (http://www3.pbs. org/weta/thewest/wpages/wpgs620/whitman1.htm). Narcissa and Marcus Whitman's efforts to set up a mission serving the Cayuse Indians at Waiilatpu in the Walla Walla Valley ends tragically in November 1847. Cultural misunderstandings and a series of unfortunate events leads to an attack on the Whitmans that results in their deaths. Narcissa Whitman's letters home offer vivid reports on frontier life.

• Museum of Westward Expansion (http://www.nps.gov/jeff/mus-tour.htm). Tour the museum exhibits on prairie schooners, buffalo, and other prominent Western symbols by clicking on the floor plan.

• Oregon-California Trails Association (http://calcite.rocky.edu/octa/octa home.htm). Preservation and education regarding the California and Oregon Trails are the primary concerns of this nonprofit organization. The gallery of trail photos, grave sites, emigrant stories, and facts are highlights of their home page.

• Oregon Trail Interpretive Center (http://www.teleport.com/~eotic/ index.html). Historical information about the role of Black Pioneers in the settlement of Oregon is very informative. Included are a timeline of events, political reactions, exclusion laws, and biographies. Another outstanding feature of this Web site is the series of articles written by Jim Thompson about the massive migration of settlers. Samples include "Outfitting for the Trail," "Life on the Trail," and "Hardships on the Oregon Trail."

- The Overland Trail (http://www.over-land.com/index.html). The Overland Trail was the route established in 1862. It avoided the Indian uprisings that were occurring on the Oregon Trail farther north. This also became the main road for the Overland Stage Company. Brief descriptions of stations, stops, and landmarks are presented along with a host of links to pioneer stories, maps, and other relevant material.

- Patrick Breen's Diary—1846 (http://www.teleport.com/%7Emhaller/Primary/BreenDiary.html). When the Donner Party became hopelessly stranded in the mountains without adequate provisions, a few of them kept diaries of the ordeal. Patrick Breen provides a daily account of the weather and the health of the people.

- Prairie Traveler (http://kuhttp.cc.ukans.edu/carrie/kancoll/books/marcy/index.html). Captain Randolph Barnes Marcy, a veteran soldier, wrote what one would consider today as the definitive guide for travel on the overland trails. He describes the advantages and disadvantages of the different routes to California and Oregon and gives practical advice on everything from daily itineraries to the treatment of rattlesnake bites.

- Trail of Hope (http://www.trailofhope.com/default.htm). Based on the PBS documentary, "Trail of Hope: The Story of the Mormon Trail," this Web site contains interesting tidbits, high-resolution graphics, and downloadable previews. You can find the story behind William Clayton's Roadmeter invention, the sites, sounds, and smells that were new to the settlers, and the pastimes of children.

- Utah: Then And Now (http://heritage.uen.org/cgi-bin/websql/classroom.hts). Exemplary lessons are designed to address the curriculum objectives across subject areas. Elementary students learn about handcarts and construct their own paper model using the online template. Secondary lessons include character sketches, a pioneer job application, and the defense of why specific items were chosen for the trek west.

# Women

- By Popular Demand: Votes for Women: Suffrage Pictures 1859–1920 (http://lcweb2.loc.gov/ammem/vfwhtml/vfwhome.html). Leaders of the suffrage movement include Cady Stanton, Julia Ward Howe, and Mary Church Terrell.

- National Women's Hall of Fame (http://www.sbaonline.sba.gov/womenin business/fame.html). Brief biographies of 125 individuals are given.

- Votes for Women: Selections from the National American Suffrage Association Collection 1848–1921 (http://lcweb2.loc.gov/ammem/naw/ naw shom.html). Explore this material from Susan B. Anthony, Carrie Chapman Catt, Julia Ward Howe, and others involved in the suffrage movement.

# STUDY AND RESEARCH SITES

- B.J. Pinchbeck's Homework Helper (http://tristate.pgh.net/~pinch13/). A student and his father, who use the Web to help with homework and research, created over 460 annotated links by subject areas.

- KidsConnect (http://www.ala.org/ICONN/Kidsconn.html). Sponsored by the American Library Association, this Web site enables students to ask questions or browse through resources.

- StudyWeb (http://www.studyweb.com). This comprehensive list of Web sites listed by subject area can be useful for completing homework assignments.

# Internet Project Ideas and Activities

Numerous Web-based resources will help teachers and students to find projects and to interact with other classrooms across the country and around the world.

## STARTING POINTS

- Global SchoolNet (http://www.gsn.org). The Global SchoolNet Foundation organizes, manages, and facilitates projects for schools. Their HILITES archives and mailing list keeps educators up-to-date on project ideas. The project registry allows schools to register upcoming events in which others might want to participate; projects range from videoconferencing to e-mail only. If you want to participate with CUSeeMe schools, there is a whole section devoted to those who have the CUSeeMe software.

- Global SchoolHouse (http://www.gsh.org). The Global SchoolHouse is part of the Global SchoolNet Organization. It is designed to build an online community.

- I*EARN (http://www.igc.org/iearn). I*EARN (International Education and Resource Network) is a nonprofit organization that creates structured projects that facilitate engaged learning and allow youth to make a difference on an International scale. Project areas include interdisciplinary topics such as the environment/science, art/literature, and social studies/politics. Some examples of past projects are the Holocaust/Genocide; the Building Wells for Clean Water in Nicaragua; and the Planetary Notions, an environmental newsletter.

- KidLink (http://www.kidlink.org/). KidLink is a nonprofit grass-roots organization aimed at getting as many young people (through age fifteen) as possible involved in a global dialog. Several languages are supported. From e-mail listservs like KidCafe to live chats to interactive projects from KidProj, this is a great gathering place for students.

- NASA's Quest Project (http://quest.arc.nasa.gov). NASA has several initiatives with education, including interactive projects utilizing distance learning, telecommunications, and collaborative efforts within the scientific community. The "Passport to Knowledge" series has been quite popular. "Live from Mars" followed the Mars Pathfinder Mission. New projects are continually being developed. Check the site for the latest project.

- OnlineClass (http://www.onlineclass.com). OnlineClass creates original K-12 programming for the Internet, delivering a planned, organized, and moderated e-mail/Web learning experience. Here you'll find live, original interactive programming materials—the "hook"—for the interdisciplinary teaching experience you want to have! Projects include Mythos: Zeus Speaks, Blue Ice: Focus on Antarctica, Rivers of Life: Mississippi Adventure, The North American Quilt: A Living Geography Project, Self*Expressing*Earth, and DoodleOpolis: Adventures in Urban Architecture. There is a nominal fee for participation.

- TEAMS Distance Learning (http://teams.lacoe.edu/documentation/projects/projects.html). The Los Angeles County Board of Education sponsors a wonderful collection of projects. These are designed by studio instructors who are interested in student collaborative work. Some examples include The Great Paper Airplane Challenge, Letters from Rifka (family stories), and Spinning Around.

- Selective Learning Network (http://www.slnedu.com). Projects such as the Virtual Senate Floor and the Peace Maker Project offer classrooms the opportunity to interact in real time online.

# PROJECT SAMPLES

- Amazing Insects (http://www.minnetonka.k12.mn.us/groveland/insect. proj/insects.html). This is an annual fall project designed for students to observe, describe, and identify insects. Interesting year-round activities are provided. One novel idea is to use recyclables to construct an insect.

- Cranes for Peace (http://www.he.net/~sparker/cranes.html). Cranes for Peace began as a project to collect paper cranes to be sent to Hiroshima for the fiftieth anniversary of the bombing. It was based on the story of Sadako Sasaki who was two at the time of the bombing. She later developed leukemia and died at the age of twelve. Sadako believed if she folded 1,000 cranes she would get well. Her story has been told in many books and serves as an inspiration for children worldwide to fold cranes for peace.

- The Global Grocery List Project (http://landmark-project.com/ggl.html). Don't have a clue about how much food costs in your town? What about in other towns around the world? Have no idea? Then, take the challenge and go on a shopping spree with the Global Grocery List Project.

- Journey North (http://www.learner.org/jnorth). Each year students and teachers follow wildlife migrations and participate in a variety of activities during Spring's Journey North and Fall's Journey South. Of particular interest is watching the migration of the monarch butterfly.

- MathMagic (http://forum.swarthmore.edu/mathmagic/index.html). Motivate students to solve math problems. Challenges in each of four categories (K-3, 4-6, 7-9, and 10-12) are designed for problem-solving dialogue between team members. When an agreement has been reached, one solution is posted for every pair. Exchanges are made through an automated list called a majordomo. A small fee of $12 is charged for each four-member team.

• Mighty M&M Math (http://mighty-mm-math.caffeinated.org/). Join in this mouth-watering project that teaches fractions and percentages. It is a wonderfully designed activity that is easy to organize and do with students. All you need are some bags of M&Ms, calculators, data tables, and a link to the Mars site.

• Postcard Geography (http://www.internet-catalyst.org/projects/PCG/post card.html). The Postcard Geography project is a really easy and fun activity to do with students. You exchange purchased or handmade cards with other classrooms and your students describe information about the geography of your area on the back of the cards. There are all sorts of tie-in activities you can do with the project.

• Westward Ho! (http://www.internet-catalyst.org/projects/WWHO/wwho. html). Load those wagons … Kiss the kin goodbye … You've decided to embark on an extraordinary adventure that will take you and your family across miles of dangerous, unfamiliar territory. You've gathered with other pioneers in Independence, Missouri. Everything that will fit inside is packed into your prairie schooner. You are as ready as you can be for the journey of nearly 2,000 miles.

# SEND A WEB POSTCARD

What a great way to complement your keypal correspondence! It's easy. Just go to any Web site in the list that follows to send colorful greetings that can be viewed using a Web browser. Want to be more creative and make your own customized cards that you can attach to e-mail messages or upload? Then, visit the Kodak site and learn how with Picture Postcard and Picture This.

- Avery Kids Sticker Buddies
  (http://www.avery.com/kids/stickerbuddy.html)

- Billy Bear's Post Office
  (http://www.billybear4kids.com/post/office.htm)

- Blue Mountain Arts' Electronic Greeting Cards
  (http://www.bluemountain.com/)

- CyberBee
  (http://www.cyberbee.com/postcards)

- Disney Cards
  http://disney.go.com/Features/Dcards/index.html

- Energizer Bunny
  http://Energizer.com/coolstuff/postcards/index.html

- Hallmark
  http://www.hallmark.com/

- Jan Brett Postcards
  (http://www.janbrett.com/postcards/cardpick_main_ choice.htm)

- Kodak Picture Postcard
  http://www.kodak.com/US/en/digital/postcard/

- Kodak Picture This (http://www.kodak.com/digitalImaging/pictureThis/ picThisHome.shtml). Kodak allows you to upload your own digital pictures and send them as a postcard. Directions are given on how to create your pictures for uploading.

- Virtual Flowers
  (http://www.virtualflowers.com)

- Warner Brothers Web Cards
  (http://rw.warnerbros.com/cmp/crd-loon.htm)

# JUST FOR FUN!

Mix frog sounds and coloring pages with dinosaur door hangers. Stir in a few beanie babies, live feeder cam shots of birds, and interactive games. What do you get? Just for Fun Web Sites!

- Banph (http://www.banph.com). Join in the adventures of Banph, the knight ant in the medieval insect kingdom.

- Barnyard Buddies (http://www.execpc.com/~byb/indexa.html). Read the Circus Champions Book, color posters, and play the Race to the Barn game. Endearing animals lead the way.

- Beanie Babies (http://www.ty.com). All of the latest news and information about Beanie Babies can be found at the Ty site.

- Ben and Jerry's Fun Stuff (http://www.benjerry.com/fun/index.html). Games, puzzles, riddles, and crafts are brought to you by Ben and Jerry along with a seasonal archive of things to do for Valentine's Day, Halloween, Thanksgiving Arts, and Winter.

- Billy Bear's Playground (http://www.billybear4kids.com). One of the coolest sites on the Internet for clip art and interactive entertainment.

- CBC 4 Kids (http://www.cbc4kids.com). The Canadian Broadcasting Company has put together a highly visual and interactive Web site that is loaded with things for kids to explore including how to make sound effects, how to write radio dramas, and how to make an indoor kite.

- Crayola (http://www.crayola.com). Learn how crayons and markers are made with an online presentation. Enter contests sponsored by the company as well as color pages, read stories, and play games.

- Garfield Online (http://www.garfield.com). Send a Garfield Postcard, play a Wacky Word Search game, read comic strips, color pictures, and enjoy the jokes.

• DK Kids (http://www.dkonline.com/dkcom/dk/1kids.html). Gather flag icons from around the world. Print out the dinosaur door hangers on a color printer, paste them on card stock, and laminate them. Kids will love hanging them on their bedroom doors.

• Froggy Page (http://frog.simplenct.com/froggy). Everything froggy from sounds to scientific information is linked.

• Headbone Zone (http://www.headbone.com). Six adventure games are employed to show students how to search and critically analyze the use of the Web while also learning about ecology, inventors, visual and performing arts, Mars, and democracy and citizenship. A teacher's guide provides further information and instructions on how to use the activities with students at different grade levels.

• Humongous Entertainment (http://www.humongous.com). Games and activities abound on this Web site.

• Judy and David Page—Online Songbook (http://judyanddavid.com). Sing-along with audio clips, and color pages from their children's album like "Froggie in the Bathtub" or "Late One Night at the Henhouse."

• Knowledge Adventure Kids (http://www.kidspace.com/kids). Search the online encyclopedia, create-a-saurus, connect the dots, and play games.

• Nabisco Kids (http://www.nabiscokids.com). You will learn everything you ever wanted to know about Oreo cookies and other Nabisco products. There are games at every turn as well as interactive features such as the writing room and the after school chat area.

• The Official Peanuts Web Site (http://www.snoopy.com/comics/peanuts). Play games, color cartoons, learn about the Peanuts characters and Charles Schultz at this delightful page.

- Wild Birds Unlimited Bird Feeder Cam (http://www.wbu.com/feedercam _home.htm). What birds visit this backyard feast? Refresh the screen and find out for yourself through the Wild Birds Unlimited Bird Feeder live cam.

# LANGUAGE ARTS ACTIVITY IDEAS

## Reach Out and Touch an Author

Children absorbed in a good book usually want to know more about the author, why certain characters were chosen, and where ideas originated to create the story. Going directly to the author is the best way to find the answers to those questions.

Before the Internet, there was little chance for interaction of any sort with an author except through a written letter to a publishing house. Now, children can correspond via e-mail, guestbooks, and forums. Although most authors do not respond individually to each letter, they do provide answers to frequently asked questions, autobiographical information, humorous thoughts, and personal touches that allow students to feel a sense of connection.

> **Send your students on an online author scavenger hunt. Use the author sites listed below.**
>
> 1. Find a photograph of Judy Blume's cabin.
> 2. What author is a pilot?
> 3. What is one thing that makes Cynthia Rylant happy?
> 4. What author trains dogs and has written essays about them?
> 5. Who wrote The Hat?
> 6. When did R.L. Stine begin writing stories?
> 7. Who wrote for Seventeen magazine during her high school years?
> 8. How did Jean Craighead George get the idea for Julie of the Wolves?
> 9. Where did Avi get his name?
> 10. Who tells frog jokes?

• AVI (http://www.avi-writer.com/). While growing up, Avi listened to radio adventures that greatly influenced his writing. In the All About My Books section, he tells interesting tidbits about the stories he has written. Ask questions and discuss topics related to Avi and his books through the online bulletin board. It can be quite fun, especially when you want to know Avi's real name.

• Judy Blume (http://www.judyblume.com/). Did you know that Judy was scared of dogs, the dark, and thunderstorms just like Sheila Tubman in *Otherwise Known as Sheila the Great*? Or that Judy's daughter took the family cat to college? These and other fascinating facts are part of the Kids area called Did You Know. Have your students sign the guestbook and read the comments others have written. All of Judy's books are listed with a brief quote. Judy also supplies funny yet candid remarks about writing.

• Jan Brett (http://www.janbrett.com/). Enter the world of Jan Brett and you won't want to leave. Not only does she share her beautiful artwork for printing, but complete background information about her books like *Armadillo Rodeo* and *Comet's Nine Lives*. Listen to her monthly hedgigram designed as a response to the e-mail letters she receives from students. Watch a delightful streaming video of Jan as she demonstrates how to draw a hedgehog. Still haven't found enough to engage your students? Then, print out the colorful masks from her books like *The Mitten* or *The Hat* and have your students act out the stories, or browse through the lessons in Piggybacks for Teachers. Jan Brett is truly a teacher's dream come true.

• Betsy Byars (http://www.betsybyars.com/). Follow Betsy's own cartoon timeline of her life. View photographs of her early years. Under the books section on the page, you can click on any title and read the plot along with commentary written by Betsy Byars, called Betsy Says. Writing tips and a guestbook are also available.

• Lois Duncan (http://www.iag.net/~barq/lois.html and http://www.random-house. com/features/loisduncan/). Although tragedy struck Lois Duncan's family in 1989 when her daughter Kaitlyn was brutally murdered, she has continued to write. Anyone who has heard her speak at conferences has learned about the parallels between the book she had just completed and her daughter's murder. Duncan kept a journal that became the book, *Who Killed My Daughter?* as the family attempted to solve the murder. Because it had no ending, her agent didn't think it could be published. When it was printed, many students thought it was fiction even without an ending. Now, there is a Web site, Who Killed Kait Arquette, devoted to solving this real-life mystery.

• Jean Craighead George (http://www.jeancraigheadgeorge.com/). Your welcome message on this page is from the author and her Alaskan Malamute, Qimmiq, via a QuickTime movie clip. In another movie segment, George describes how she approaches her writing in the morning. You can listen to a couple of audio clips taken from *One Day in the Woods*, a release by Harper Children's Audio and based on George's book of the same title. For students, she gives hints on how to work through the writing process. Her entire book list is linked to Amazon.com for easy ordering.

• Virginia Hamilton (http://www.virginiahamilton.com). Did you know Virginia Hamilton collects frogs? Visit her Web site and contribute a frog joke or listen to hers. Hamilton's personality certainly shines through as she tells her own story and describes a picture taken of her at age five. You can also find the latest about her books and upcoming publications. Be sure to e-mail her at bodeep@aol.com.

• Daniel Pinkwater (http://www.designfoundry.com/p-zone/). At The (sort of) Official Daniel Pinkwater Web site, tongue-in-cheek humor rules. Outrageously funny, Daniel Pinkwater responds to forum mail, a good place to follow all kinds of dialogue. There are RealAudio excerpts from Dog Essays, sound clips for your Macintosh or Windows computer, and a list of Pinkwater's books.

• Cynthia Rylant (http://www.rylant.com/). From picture books to novels to nonfiction, Cynthia Rylant crosses all generations with her wonderful stories. Her words about her childhood and how she became a writer are an inspiration to aspiring writers. View her scrapbook and the myriad of pets that occupy her home in Eugene, Oregon. Her personal message will warm your heart.

• R. L. Stine (http://www.scholastic.com/Goosebumps/high/stine/). Graves come to life as you roll your mouse across the foreboding tombstones. It is a clever navigation trick for Stine's Web site. His immensely popular scary stories serve as the backdrop for some great activities at the Goosebumps fun house. You'll never look at your hand in the same way after you engage in palm reading. Kids will love whipping up a batch of slimy stretchy stuff to squeeze and bounce. A brief biography about the author and a comprehensive list of his books round out the page.

## Pop-Up Books

Here are activities you could incorporate into your language arts curriculum. Have your students read *How a Book Is Made* by Aliki at the HarperCollins Web site. Then, print out the Noodles pop-up book page at the same location. Have your students color the picture with magic markers or crayons. Then cut, paste, and fold to make the book. Take the activity one step further by having students create their own pop-ups and stories. The following listing points you to some terrific pages that can help you get started.

• Concise History of Pop-Up Books—Ann Montanaro
  (http://www. libraries.rutgers.edu/rulib/spcol/montanar/p-intro.htm)

• HarperCollins Big Busy House
  (http://www.harperchildrens.com)

• History of Pop-Up Books
  (http://www.bookwire.com/pw/asia/popohist.html)

• How a Book Is Made
  (http://www.harperchildrens.com/howabook/index.htm)

- How to Make a Pop-Up—Joan Irvine
  (http://www.makersgallery. com/joanirvine/)

- Noodles
  (http://www.harperchildrens.com/howabook/nooind.htm)

# Unleash Creative Talents

Capture your daydreamers and their imaginations by immersing them in creative enterprises. Grab those crayons, watercolors, and computer paint programs. Turn on video cameras and audio recorders. Plug in the writing process. Organize your action plan. Then, hold onto your seats as original art, ghostly tales, hilarious banter, dramatic dialogue, and breathtaking adventures flow from the minds of your students. Whatever they create, one thing is certain, they will remember the experience forever.

Are you working on a publishing project in your classroom? Do your students enjoy the arts? Do you need ideas and ways to generate enthusiasm? From imagination to expression, these selected sites will help you begin to unleash the creative writing and artistic talents of your students.

## Writing Process

- Silly Billy's World (http://www.sillybilly.com). Start with the Silly Billy home page where author/illustrator Bill Dallas Lewis shares how to write and publish a book.

- Big Busy House (http://www.harperchildrens.com). HarperCollins created the Big Busy House to feature authors and their works. Let Aliki, author of *How a Book Is Made*, take you through the ten stages of bookmaking.

- Inkspot (http://www.inkspot.com). A trip to Inkspot will provide a wealth of information for middle and high school students.

- Nebraska Center for Writers (http://mockingbird.creighton.edu/NCW). Aspiring teen authors will find the Nebraska Center for Writers to be a great starting point. It is chock-full of resources. Writing guides from character development to critiquing poetry provide important tips and hints.

• Scriptito's Place—Vangar Publisher (http://members.aol.com/vanga rnews /scriptito.html). Once in a while you will find a hidden gem on the Internet. Scriptito's Place is one of those jewels. It may not be glitzy, but the rich content written by Dr. Virginia Lynch Graf is very practical for teachers to use.

## Artistry at Work

• Cartoon Mania (http://www.worldchat.com/public/jhish/cartoon.html). If you are not artistically inclined, head straight for Cartoon Mania—brought to you from the pen of Jerry Hish. Learn to draw any of four funny animals. Materials are listed along with illustrated directions. Be prepared for the corny jokes that greet you at the end of each lesson.

• Warner Brothers—Animation 101 (http://www.wbanimation.com/cmp/ ani_04if.htm). Follow the step-by-step process of writers and artists as they create an animated cartoon from storyboard to finished product.

• DC Comics (http://www.dccomics.com). One way to spark interest in writing is to have students create their own scripts, act out the parts, use sound effects, and record the production. Blast into the past on the DC Comics home page to hear an old-time radio program.

• Radio Days (http://www.otr.com). Are your students curious about classic radio programs beyond the comics? Would you like to reset the clock to the 1930s and 1940s? Have your students visit those thrilling days of yesteryear by stopping off at Radio Days. It is a treasure trove of clips and descriptions from a variety of shows.

## Publishing on the Web

- CyberKids—Cyberteens (http://www.cyberkids.com). Winner of numerous Web awards, CyberKids is the online home for KidZeen. Mountain Lake Software, Inc. of San Francisco, California, publishes it four times a year. Their goal is to create and promote youth community worldwide and give kids a voice and an interactive place to express their creativity.

- KidPub (http://www.kidpub.org). KidPub is a corner of the World Wide Web where children are encouraged to publish stories and news about their schools and towns.

- MidLink (http://longwood.cs.ucf.edu/~MidLink). MidLink is a quarterly electronic magazine for students aged ten to fifteen. It is sponsored by the North Carolina Department of Public Instruction, North Carolina State University, and the University of Central Florida. Collaborative projects are featured in addition to ongoing activities.

- Teen Voices @ Teen Link (http://www.nypl.org/branch/teen/teenlink.html). Original poetry or short stories written by young people between the ages of twelve and eighteen can be sent to the New York Public Library's Teen Voices. It is open to teenagers everywhere.

# MATH ACTIVITY IDEAS

## Bubble Geometry

Have you ever wondered whether you can blow square bubbles? Using bubble mix and pipe cleaners, find out the answer to this question and others through hands-on experimentation.

- Amazing Bubbles
  (http://www.best.com/~zometool/bubblehome/bubblehow/index.html)

• Bubble Geometry—Science Museum of Minnesota
(http://www.sci.mus.mn.us/sln/tf/b/bubblegeometry/bubblegeometry.html)

• Bubbles—Exploratorium
(http://www.exploratorium.edu/ronh/bubbles/bubbles.html)

• Bubbles—Science World
(http://www.rescol.ca/collections/science_world/english/projects/activities/
bubbles.html)

## M&M Math

Can you guess how many M&Ms are in a bag? What is the probability of the same number of colors in each bag? The next time your students complain that math is boring, toss them a bag of M&Ms.

• M&M Math (http://ericir.syr.edu/Virtual/Lessons/Mathematics/Arithmetic/
ATH0015.html). Prepare and eat M&M cookies. In the process, tally the number of colors found in each cookie. A simple computation sheet is used to determine who has the most valuable cookie.

• M&M Project (http://www.minnetonka.k12.mn.us/support/science/les
sons45/mandm.html). Here is a really nice worksheet to use with students in Grades 4–5. It even has a place for the parent's signature where he or she can get involved as well.

• M&M's Studios (http://www.baking.m-ms.com/). Lots of baking recipes and information on the M&M stars are provided at this site.

• M&Ms Line Plots and Graphing (http://www.kings.k12.ca.us/math/lessons/
mms.htm). Here are work sheets to use with your lessons, plus suggested extensions with Graphpower. Grades 3–4.

# Science Activity Ideas

## Flying Free—Paper Airplane Science

Let your budding pilots test paper airplane designs and record data using the Paper Airplane Science lesson. Then graph the results. You will be amazed.

- Aviation Education—Minnesota Department of Transportation
  (http://www.dot.state.mn.us/aeronautics/AVEDU/CURRICULA/lessons.html)

- BAD Web (Basic Aircraft Design)
  (http://fornax.arc.nasa.gov:9999/bad web/badweb.html)

- Build the Best Paper Airplane in the World
  (http://www.zurqui.com/crinfocus/paper/airplane.html)

- Great Paper Airplane Challenge
  (http://teams.lacoe.edu/documentation/projects/math/airplane.html)

- Paper Airplane Hanger
  (http://www.cs.man.ac.uk/~yeomansb/planes)

- Paper Airplanes—Quick and Simple
  (http://www.onenorthpole.com/ToyShop/Paperairplanes.html)

- Unusual Paper Airplane—Using a Straw and Paper
  (http://www.dot.state.mn.us/aeronautics/AVEDU/PUBLICATIONS/SKY
  SLIM3/air plane.html)

- World Record Paper Airplane
  (http://www.workman.com/plane.html)

- Paper Airplane Aerodynamics
  (http://www.geocities.com/CapeCanaveral/1817/paero.html)

- Wing Design and Aspect Ratio
  (http://ldaps.ivv.nasa.gov/Curriculum/Curriculum/Wing-design.html)

• Paper Airplane Science—Lesson Plan
  (http://explorer.scrtec.org/explorer/explorer-db/html/
    783750895-447DED81.html)

# Space ... The Final Frontier— Land Rovers on the Move

Study the Mars Pathfinder mission. Have your students build the Pathfinder Spacecraft Model.

• Build Your Own Mars Pathfinder Spacecraft Model
  (http://mars.jpl.nasa.gov/MPF/mpf/education/cutouts.html)

• Mars Pathfinder
  (http://mars.jpl.nasa.gov/MPF/index0.html)

• NASA's Quest Project—K-12 Interactive Initiatives
  (http://quest.arc.nasa.gov)

• Nine Planets
  (http://seds.lpl.arizona.edu/nineplanets/nineplanets/nineplanets.html)

• Welcome to the Planets
  (http://pds.jpl.nasa.gov/planets)

# Additional Space Web Sites

• Earth Viewer
  (http://www.fourmilab.ch/earthview/vplanet.html)

• Eye on the Universe The Hubble Space Telescope
  (http://www.thetech.org/hyper/hubble)

- Liftoff to Space Exploration
  (http://liftoff.msfc.nasa.gov)

- NASA SpaceLink
  (http://spacelink.nasa.gov/.index.html)

- Space Calendar
  (http://www.jpl.nasa.gov/calendar/)

- Space Curriculum—Athena
  (http://athena.wednet.edu/curric/space/index.html)

- Windows to the Universe
  (http://www.windows.umich.edu)

# Schoolyard Science—
# Making a Weather Station

The following sites have information for weather units. You will also find activities that will allow you to create your own weather monitoring instruments using household materials.

- A to Z Weather Index—USA Today (http://www.usatoday.com/weather/windex.htm). It's like having a weather encyclopedia online. The site has a great number of illustrations and animations.

- Dan's Wild Wild Weather Page (http://www.whnt19.com/kidwx/index.html). Good starting point for students to learn about weather.

- FEMA for Kids (http://www.fema.gov/kids). A really cool site on preparing for disaster. Interactive coloring pages, jokes, and stories are some of the features.

- Franklin Science Institute (http://sln.fi.edu/weather). Learn how to make weather instruments.

• Miami Museum of Science Making a Weather Station (http://www.miami sci.org/hurricane/weatherstation.html). Step-by-step instructions on making weather instruments.

• Observing the Weather Today—(KidPix) for Grades K-4—Athena (http://athena.wednet.edu/curric/weather/calendar.kpx). This is a really neat graphic that you can use with KidPix to create your own weekly forecasts.

• Rain or Shine (http://www.rainorshine.com). Your elementary students will find Rain or Shine very easy to use. Simply choose the city and submit the request for an instant five-day forecast.

• Weather Calculator (http://nwselp.epcc.edu/elp/wxcalc.html). Go here for online conversions for temperature, heat index, wind chill, and more.

• Weather Channel—Learn More
(http://www.weather.com/)

• Weather Curriculum—Athena (Grades K-12)
(http://athena.wednet.edu/curric/weather/index.html)

• Weather Dude (http://www.nwlink.com/~wxdude). Sing along with the Weather Dude, Nick Walker. His irresistible recordings and lyrics give a musical twist to meteorology.

• Weather Folklore Lesson (http://www.athena.ivv.nasa.gov/curric/weather/ hsweathr/folktale.html). This site contains an excellent lesson and links for weather wisdom and folklore.

• Weather Here and There (http://www.ncsa.uiuc.edu/Edu/RSE/RSEred/ WeatherHome.html). Six lessons incorporating math, science, geography, and language arts make up this collaborative unit on weather for elementary students.

• Weather Underground (http://groundhog.sprl.umich.edu/). This is the home of Blue Skies, software for elementary students to use in the study of weather. In addition, a list of weather cams will give you real-time observations in many cities around the country.

- WSFO Louisville, Kentucky: CONVERT (http://www.crh.noaa.gov/ lmk/news.htm). A cool weather conversion program for Windows 95, it's a must-have and it's free!

# Rain Forest Music

Using the broad theme of Rain Forest Music, have your students discover this interesting ecosystem. Use these questions for their exploration: (1) Find out what plants and animals live in the rain forest. Choose a plant or animal to investigate. Write a short report on your findings and include a picture. (2) What sights and sounds will you encounter? Take a musical journey through the rain forest.

- Amazon Interactive (http://www.eduweb.com/amazon.html). Explore the geography of the Ecuadorian Amazon through online games and activities. Learn about the rain forest and the Quichua people who call it home. Discover the ways in which the Quichua live off the land. Then try your hand at running a community-based ecotourism project along the Río Napo.

- Indonesian Tropical Rain Forest (http://www.geocities.com/RainForest/ 3678). Journey through an Indonesian rain forest. (Note that information had not been updated since 1996 at the time of this writing.)

- KidsQuest Rain Forest (http://www.christiananswers.net/kids/kidshome. html). Experience beautiful photographs, sounds, and activities.

- Lesson Plan for How to Make a Rainstick (http://ericir.syr.edu/Virtual/ Lessons/Science/Earth/EAR0033.html). This lesson plan includes a poem.

- Rain Forest Action Network (http://www.ran.org). This terrific page of information will stimulate discussion on current issues as well as provide facts about the habitat.

- The Rain Forest Workshop (http://kids.osd.wednet.edu/Marshall/rainforest_home_page.html). This is a good starting point for your classroom study, with lots of resources and samples of student work.

- STOMP (http://www.stomponline/). Visit this excellent source for lessons on music, for directions on how to make musical instruments, and for the sounds of the rain forest. Don't miss this site if you are planning a unit on the rain forest.

- The Toucan Sam Rain Forest Encyclopedia (http://www.toucansam.com). Let Toucan Sam show you examples of plants, animals, and people of the rain forest ecosystem.

# Schoolyard Science— Design a Butterfly Garden

Using the Web sites listed here, explore the world of butterflies, then design a garden for them to enjoy.

- Butterfly Web Site (http://www.mgfx.com/butterfly/). Visit here for butterfly house plans and landscaping suggestions.

- Butterfly World
  (http://www.butterflyworld.com)

- Monarch Watch—Butterfly Gardening (http://www.monarchwatch.org/). Read about butterfly house plans and information on Monarch butterflies here.

- Territorial Seed Company (http://www.territorial-seed.com). Send for seeds for your butterfly garden.

- Welcome to Pennington Seed (http://www.penningtonseed.com/index.html). Use this site to get seeds for your butterfly garden.

- Wildflowers in Bloom (http://aggie-horticulture.tamu.edu/wildseed). Wildflowers in Bloom is a cooperative project between Wildseed Farms and the Texas Horticulture Program. This page could easily serve as an online field guide with its lavish images, distribution range map, and growing information.

# SOCIAL STUDIES ACTIVITY IDEAS

## Country Journey

In this activity, you will be creating a travel brochure. You may use any word processing or publishing program. In fact, you could design a Web page with the country information. Be sure to include the flag, map, common phrases, currency and its equivalent in dollars, ways to travel to this destination, a description of the country, things to do, and any other interesting tidbits you might learn. Use the following Web sites to help you.

- 1998 World Factbook (http://www.odci.gov/cia/publications/factbook/index.html). Country information is compiled and published by the CIA.

- All of the Embassies of Washington D.C. (http://www.embassy.org/embassies/eep-1100.html). Alphabetical listing includes address, phone number, and any Web links.

- Around the World in 80 Clicks (http://www.steveweb.com/80clicks/). This has links to tourist information.

- Currency Converter (http://www.oanda.com/converter/classic). This converts 164 currencies using an easy interactive form.

- The Embassy Page (http://www.embpage.org). Use these addresses and contact information for embassies around the world.

- Flags of All Countries (http://www.wave.net/upg/immigration/flags.html). Color country flags.

- Foreign Languages for Travelers (http://www.travlang.com/languages). Common phrases travelers use are presented.

- Yahooligans Countries (http://www.yahooligans.com/Around_the_World/ Countries). The site provides links to lots of country sites.

# Culture Capsule

Explore a Day in the Life of Thomas Jefferson, then compare and contrast a day in the 1990s. Decorate a shoe box and create a culture time capsule. For example, what kind of writing instrument did Jefferson use? What do we use today? There are many things that you can read about at this Web site. It is brimful of pictures and descriptions.

- Monticello—Home of Thomas Jefferson
  (http://www.monticello.org)

# Here Come the Cybercasters

Plan, gather, and write a morning news broadcast that will last approximately ten minutes. You may want to divide the group into career roles, such as news anchor, producer, technical director, and field reporters.

- KidNews (http://www.kidnews.com/). KidNews is a place to publish student writing.

# Some Additional Suggestions

Create a newspaper Web page for the school, including a JavaScript ticker tape. Create RealAudio broadcasts for the school Web page. Use these news and media Web sites to gather information:

- ABC News
  (http://www.abcnews.com)

- Boston Globe Online
  (http://www.boston.com/globe)

- CBS News
  (http://www.cbs.com/navbar/news.html)

- CNN
  (http://www.cnn.com)

- CNN Newsroom
  (http://cnn.com/CNN/Programs/CNNnewsroom)

- MSNBC
  (http://www.msnbc.com/news)

- Reuters
  (http://www.reuters.com)

- Sports Illustrated for Kids
  (http://www.sikids.com/)

- This Day in History
  (http://www.historychannel.com/thisday)

- Time for Kids
  (http://www.pathfinder.com/TFK)

- Today in History
  (http://lcweb2.loc.gov/today/today.html)

- U.S. News Online
  (http://www.usnews.com/usnews/home.htm)

- USA Today
  (http://www.usatoday.com/)

- Yak's Corner (Detroit Free Press)
  (http://www.yakscorner.com/)

- Weather Channel
  (http://www.weather.com)

# READY REFERENCE SCAVENGER HUNT

Have fun trying to find the solutions to these reference questions. Go to the suggested Web site and search for the answer. You may also want to search pages such as Lycos, Infoseek, or Yahoo!. You are a Cybernaut if you can find 17–20 answers, an Internet Navigator with 13–16, a Hitchhiker with 9–12, or a Newbie with less than 9:

1. What words are similar in meaning to run?
   Hint: Roget's Thesaurus
       (http://humanities.uchicago.edu/forms_unrest/ ROGET.html)

2. What play contains these famous lines? "Double, double toil and trouble; Fire burn, and cauldron bubble."
       Hint: Project Bartleby
           (http://www.columbia.edu/acis/bartleby/bartlett/)

3. How do you say "nice to meet you" in Dutch?
   Hint: Foreign Languages for Travelers
       (http://www.travlang.com/lang uages/)

4. What is the toll free number for Compaq Computers?
   Hint: AT&T 800 Toll-Free Internet Directory
       (http://www.att.net/find/tf.html)

5. How many degrees Celsius equals 85 degrees Fahrenheit?
   Hint: The Weather Calculator
       (http://nwselp.epcc.edu/elp/wxcalc.html)

6. What is the current trading price for the maker of Big Macs?
   Hint: Infoseek: Stock Quotes
   (http://money.go.com/)

7. January 1, 2000 will fall on what day of the week?
   Hint: WWW Calendar Generator
   (http://www.inet-images.com/manny/cal2htm.htm)

8. What happened on April 1 in history?
   Hint: Today in History—History Channel
   (http://www.historychannel.com/tdih/index.html)

9. What is the address for the Chinese Embassy in Washington, D.C.?
   Hint: All of the D.C. Embassies
   (http://www.embassy.org/embassies)

10. A vexillologist is what kind of expert?
    Hint: Betsy Ross home page
    (http://www.libertynet.org/iha/betsy)

11. Where would you find a topographical map of Colorado? Find and print it.
    Hint: Color Landform Atlas of the United States
    (http://fermi.jhuapl.edu/states)

12. Where would you find a map of the North Pole? Find and print it.
    Hint: Getting Around the Planet
    (http://pathfinder.com/travel)

13. Who is the current ruler of the Ukraine?
    Hint: Rulers
    (http://www.geocities.com/Athens/1058/rulers.html)

14. What is the current United States population?
    Hint: U.S. Census Bureau Home Page
    (http://www.census.gov)

15. Who are the two senators from Oregon in the 105th Congress?

    Hint: Thomas Legislative Online

    (http://thomas.loc.gov)

16. Where can you find a copy of the First Thanksgiving Proclamation?
    What is the date on the document?

    Hint: University of Oklahoma Historical Documents

    (http://www.law.ou.edu/hist/)

17. What are the do's and don'ts of taking medicine?

    Hint: HealthTouch Online

    (http://www.healthtouch.com)

18. When was Bill Clinton born?

    Hint: Biography

    (http://www.biography.com)

19. Who is Kathleen Battle?

    Hint: Mr. ShowBiz Star CelebSite

    (http://www.celebsite.com)

20. Where can you go for the latest headlines and global news coverage?
    What is happening today?

    Hint: Reuters News Room

    (http://www.reuters.com/news)

# BELLS AND WHISTLES ON THE WEB

The following Web sites are illustrations of the effective ways in which multimedia can be used on the Internet.

• American Memory Collection (http://lcweb2.loc.gov/ammem). Visit the Learning Page (http://lcweb2.loc.gov/ammem/ndlpedu/index.html). You can put together a shockwave puzzle picture taken from the American Memory Collection at the Library of Congress.

• Dinosaur Eggs—National Geographic (http://www.nationalgeographic.com/dinoeggs/index.html). View QuickTime VR rendered dinosaur embryos.

• A Visit to Capitol Square (http://www.statehouse.state.oh.us). Another example of QTVR is a 360-degree view of the Ohio statehouse rotunda. On the main page, click on View QTVR and select Rotunda.

• Weather Cam (http://cirrus.sprl.umich.edu/wxnet/wxcam.html). One example of a live camera shot can be obtained from San Francisco's KGO-TV's SFO-Live Cam, which is updated every fifteen minutes. The Snappy camera and software are used to shoot the picture and transfer the file via FTP. Live cams provide another dimension to the Web. One of the most interesting live cam examples was the Peregrine Falcon Hatching sponsored by the Ohio Division of Wildlife. You could watch the baby chicks hatch and then learn to fly.

• Poetry and Music of the War Between the States (http://www.erols.com/kfraser). This is an example of the use of midi files on the Web.

• Carlos' Coloring Book (http://coloring.com/). One of the first interactive sites on the Web was a coloring page that utilized CGI (Common Gateway Interface) scripting. It redraws the picture with the new color added. You can save your finished picture to a disk or your hard drive as an image file. Import the image into your favorite paint program and print it on a color printer. Another use would be to include it in a project report.

• Biography (http://www.biography.com). View and listen to video streaming using RealPlayer.

# Chapter 4

# Copyright and Property Rights

Everything on the Net is public domain. Right? Read "The 10 Big Myths About Copyright Explained" by Brad Templeton and you will soon have a different perspective. Another thought-provoking article is David H. Rothman's "Copyright and K-12: Who Pays in the Network Era?" His premise is that, with the current law, children may pay the ultimate price because inadequate budgets will not allow schools to pay licensing fees. Several issues are presented: what networks mean to teachers and students, how copyright may affect K-12 networking, the attitudes of educators, and the options for a solution.

For basic copyright information, current legislation, and international agreements go to the United States Copyright Office. The Copyright Clearance Center is a not-for-profit organization created to help organizations comply with U.S. copyright law. With over 1.75 million titles, it provides authorized users with a lawful means to make photocopies. For guidelines on what you may copy as a teacher, read "Reproduction of Copyrighted Works by Educators and Librarians" at the Library of Congress. A more recent document, "Fair Use Guidelines for Educational Multimedia," adopted by the House Judiciary Subcommittee on Courts and Intellectual Property in September 1996, can be found at the Consortium for College and University Media Centers, Indiana University.

## COPYRIGHT AND FAIR USE REFERENCES

- Chang, Christopher; Herskowitz, Scott; Lee, Sang T.; and Carter Page. Intellectual Property in the Information Age, [Online]. Available: World Wide Web: http://homepage.seas.upenn.edu/~cpage/cis590.

- Copyright Clearance Center. [Online]. Available: World Wide Web: http://www.copyright.com.

- Sivin, J.P. and Bialo, E.R. 1992. Ethical Use of Information Technologies in Education (Issues and Practices). 34 pp. NCJ 136548. $10.50 (U.S), $15.00 (Canada), $15.50 (Other Countries).

- Fair Use Guidelines for Educational Media. [Online]. Available: World Wide Web: http://www.indiana.edu/~ccumc/mmfairuse.html.

- O'Mahoney, P.J. Benedict. (1995). Copyright Fundamentals, [Online]. Available: World Wide Web: http://www.benedict.com/.

- Reproduction of Copyrighted Works by Educators and Librarians. [Online]. Available: World Wide Web: http://lcweb.loc.gov/copyright/circs/circ21.pdf.

- Rothman, David. (1996, May 1). Copyright and K-12: Who Pays in the Network Era?, [Online]. Available: World Wide Web: http://www.ed.gov/Technology/Futures/rothman.html.

- Templeton, Brad. 10 Big Myths About Copyright Explained, [Online]. Available: World Wide Web: http://www.clari.net/brad/copymyths.html.

- U.S. Copyright Office. [Online]. Available: World Wide Web: http://lcweb.loc.gov/copyright.

# WEB BUDDY

Web Buddy is a set of utilities that allows you to collect, schedule, convert, and organize Web pages using a Web browser like Netscape or Internet Explorer. Trial versions are available for downloading.

DataViz Products

(http://www.dataviz.com/products/webbuddy)

| | |
|---|---|
| Platform: | Macintosh 68K |
| | Macintosh PPC |
| | Windows 95 |
| Price: | $39.95 |
| Phone: | (800) 733-0030 |
| E-mail: | Info@dataviz.com |

# WEBWHACKER

WebWhacker is a product that allows you to download Web pages to a hard drive. A table of contents is created to make launching the pages a mouse click away. Version 1.0 is actually easier to use than the newer versions, but there is a learning curve involved. Knowing HTML makes using WebWhacker more user-friendly. Demos are available to download.

Blue Squirrel

http://www.bluesquirrel.com/whacker

| | |
|---|---|
| Platform: | Macintosh 68K |
| | Macintosh PPC |
| | Windows95/NT |
| | Windows 3.1 |
| Price: | $49.95 |
| Phone: | (800) 403-0925 |
| | (801) 523-1063 |
| E-mail: | sales@bluesquirrel.com |

# OFF-LINE CAPTURING USING NETSCAPE COMMUNICATOR 4.0

Using Netscape Communicator for Web page capture is an excellent method when you simply want to download one page to use in the classroom.

1. Copy the URL (address) you want to download.

2. Go to "File" and select "Open Location" in Composer.

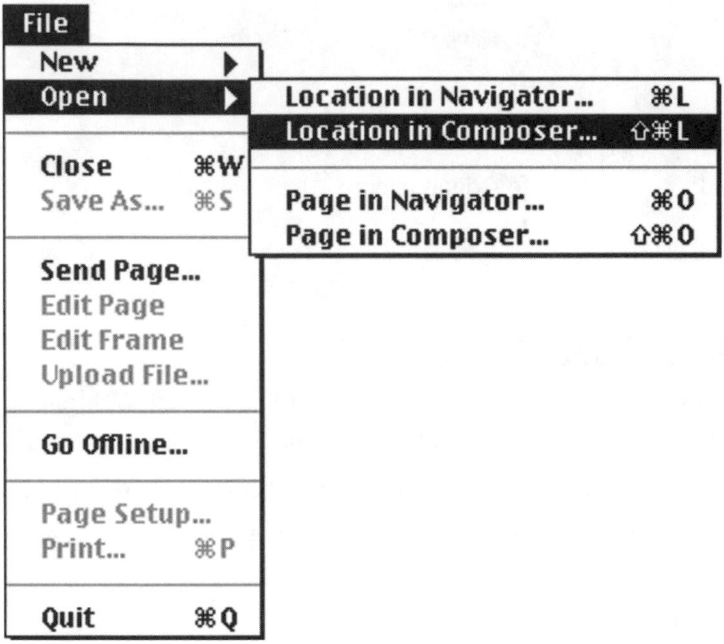

| File | | |
|------|---|---|
| **New** | ▶ | |
| **Open** | ▶ | **Location in Navigator...**   ⌘L |
| | | **Location in Composer...**   ⇧⌘L |
| **Close**   ⌘W | | |
| Save As...   ⌘S | | **Page in Navigator...**   ⌘O |
| | | **Page in Composer...**   ⇧⌘O |
| **Send Page...** | | |
| Edit Page | | |
| Edit Frame | | |
| Upload File... | | |
| **Go Offline...** | | |
| Page Setup... | | |
| Print...   ⌘P | | |
| **Quit**   ⌘Q | | |

*FIGURE 4.3*

3. When the dialog box opens, type or paste in the URL.

Click on "Open." The page will appear in the Composer window.

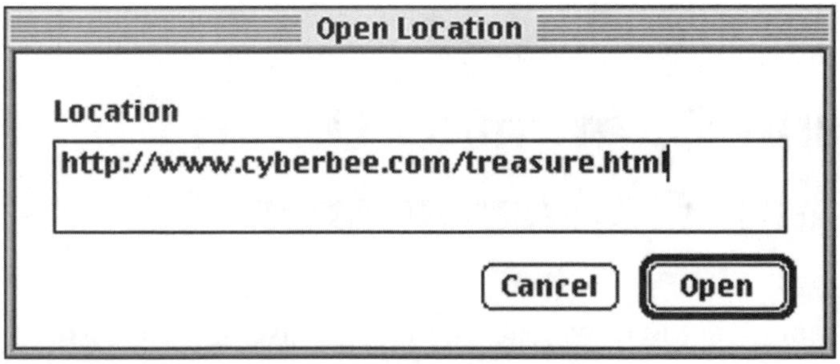

**Open Location**

**Location**

`http://www.cyberbee.com/treasure.html`

( Cancel ) [ **Open** ]

*FIGURE 4.4*

4. Go to "File" and select "Save As."

**FIGURE 4.5**

5. A message will appear warning you that you are about to download files on a remote server and you should get permission for any copyrighted material. You have the option of not having the message appear again or clicking on "Okay."

**FIGURE 4.6**

6. A dialog box will open with a filename. You will want to save it to a folder so the file and images are easy to find; otherwise, they might end up in your Netscape folder or elsewhere, depending on how your preferences are set. Create a new folder and give it the name of the site or something you will remember. Click on "Create."

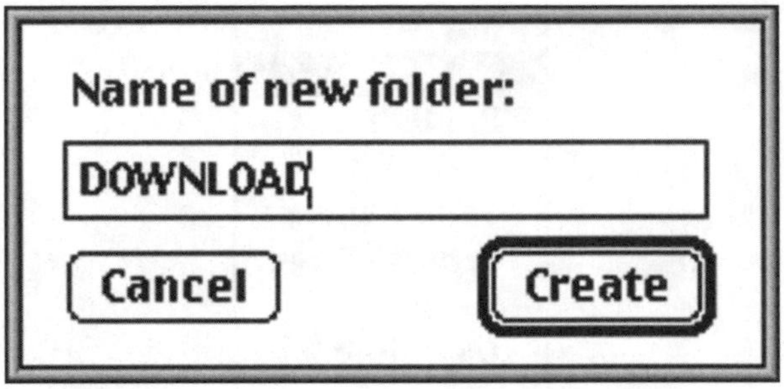

**FIGURE 4.7**

7. Save the page in the new folder you created. Click on "Save."

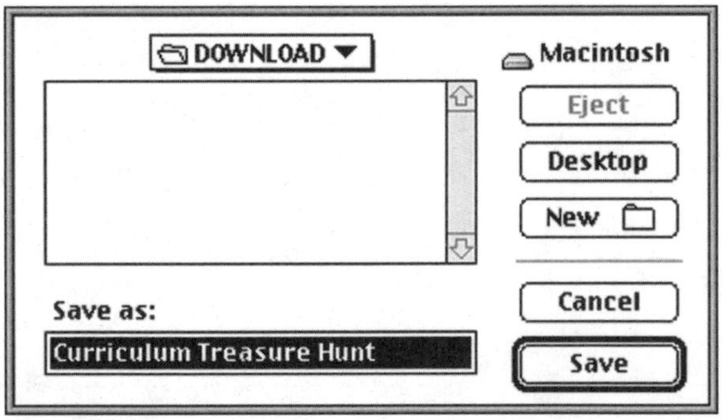

**FIGURE 4.8**

8. To open the page you downloaded, go to "File" and select "Open Page" in Navigator. Find the page you downloaded and click on open. The page should appear intact with the images, etc.; however, I tried the same procedure with one of the HyperNews pages and some of the images were missing. I tried it with other pages and it worked fine. In other words, sometimes it will work and other times it will not, depending on how files are organized and stored on the server.

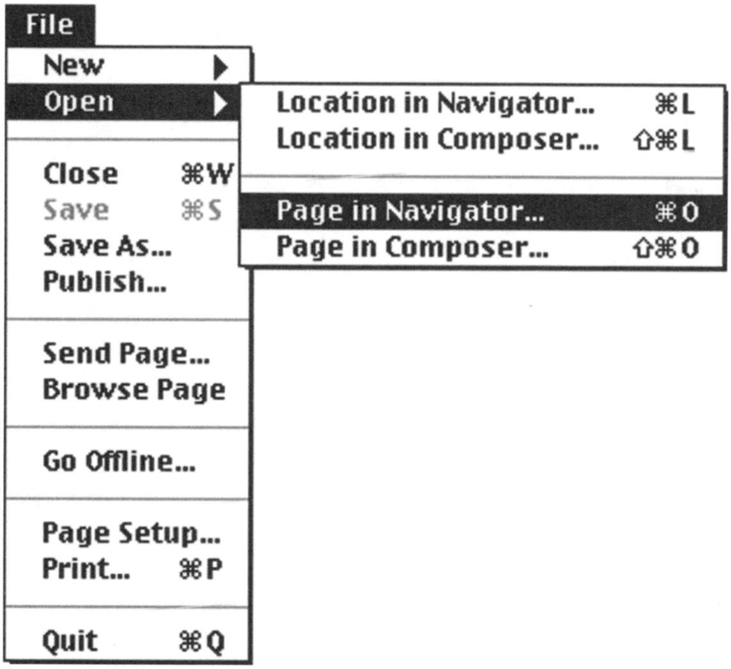

| File | | |
|---|---|---|
| New | ▶ | |
| Open | ▶ | Location in Navigator... ⌘L |
| | | Location in Composer... ⇧⌘L |
| Close | ⌘W | |
| Save | ⌘S | Page in Navigator... ⌘O |
| Save As... | | Page in Composer... ⇧⌘O |
| Publish... | | |
| Send Page... | | |
| Browse Page | | |
| Go Offline... | | |
| Page Setup... | | |
| Print... | ⌘P | |
| Quit | ⌘Q | |

*FIGURE 4.9*

# Chapter 5

# Acceptable Use and Student Safety

Have you ever been spammed with advertising sent to everyone on the listserv? These may be intrusive messages but really cause no harm unless they are sent in such quantity that they shut down an Internet Service Provider's system. When school networks become homes to e-mail accounts for teachers and students, who will be responsible for the e-mail sent over those data lines?

Try typing this address: http://www.whitehouse.com. You'll find that it isn't the White House—it's a pornographic site. The difference is the domain name at the end: The real White House site is at http://www.whitehouse.gov. Notice the difference between ".gov" and ".com." It would be easy to make this mistake when typing an Internet address.

So the questions are, what measures will school administrators be able to take with an employee or student if they use the Net for inappropriate or noneducational purposes? Who will police students and teachers? How do First Amendment rights apply to the Internet? These are burning issues that might convince a board of education to simply ban Internet use in its school system altogether.

## ACCEPTABLE USE

Nancy Willard, an educational consultant with a law degree from Willamette University, has written a detailed legal analysis of acceptable use policies and provides a framework for districts to follow. It is written in easy-to-understand language, and you will want to thoroughly digest these documents before you write your school's policy. The entire group of templates from broad statement to the student/parent agreement form are available for a licensing fee of $50. This is a real bargain when you consider the amount of time you would spend creating one from scratch.

Other examples of school acceptable use policies can be accessed at the Armadillo's WWW Server. For kid safety check out Lawrence Magid's Safe Kids Online Web site. He wrote the Child Safety on the Information Highway pamphlet that is being distributed by the National Center for Missing and Exploited Children. You can read and print a copy from this page. A tear-off page, My Rules for Online Safety, can be kept at the computer. Disney created a neat multimedia presentation, "CyberNetiquette Comix," based on the story of the *Three Little Pigs*. Younger kids will enjoy this interactive way to learn about online safety. These useful sites are as follows:

- K-12 Acceptable Use Policies—Nancy Willard
  (http://www.erehwon.com/k12aup/)

- Armadillo
  (http://chico.rice.edu/armadillo/Rice/Resources/acceptable.html)

- CyberNetiquette Comix
  (http://www.disney.com/CyberNetiquette/)

- Safe Kids Online
  (http://www.safekids.com/)

# Nancy Willard's K-12 Acceptable Use Policies

*The Acceptable Use Policy and Student Account Agreement template that follow are reprinted with permission from K-12 Acceptable Use Policies (http://www.erehwon.com/k12aup/); by Nancy Willard, Information Technology Consultant; Internet: nwillard@ordata.com.*

# Acceptable Use Policy Template

## *Information About Use of Materials on This Site*

The materials on this site are protected by copyright. The author grants permission for districts and others to download the materials for review. Public school districts and private, non-profit schools may modify these materials and reproduce them for use in their schools. However, if districts or schools use the materials in this manner, they must pay the author a licensing fee in the amount of $50 (for the entire set of templates). All other copyright rights are retained by the author. Districts may electronically request an invoice through this site.

The use of information technologies to provide access to information and materials will require us to develop new ways of providing compensation to those individuals who create works of value. The materials on this site are being provided under the assumption that if districts and schools find they are of value, they will provide proper compensation.

The author intends to use the income received from the distribution of these materials to support additional development of materials and learning activities that address the effective and ethical use of the Internet in our classrooms. You may contact the author for further information.

## *Student Acceptable Use Policy Template*

* School District is now offering Internet access for student use. This document contains the Acceptable Use Policy for your use of * (system).

### A. Educational Purpose

1. * (system) has been established for a limited educational purpose. The term "educational purpose" includes classroom activities, career development, and limited high-quality self-discovery activities.

2. * (system) has not been established as a public access service or a public forum. * (district) has the right to place reasonable restrictions on the material you access or post through the system. You are also expected to follow the rules set forth in * (disciplinary code) and the law in your use of * (system).

3. You may not use * (system) for commercial purposes. This means you may not offer, provide, or purchase products or services through * (system).

4. You may not use * (system) for political lobbying. But you may use the system to communicate with elected representatives and to express your opinion on political issues.

## B. Student Internet Access

1. All students will have access to Internet World Wide Web information resources through their classroom, library, or school computer lab.

2. Elementary students will have e-mail access only under their teacher's direct supervision using a classroom account. Elementary students may be provided with individual e-mail accounts under special circumstances, at the request of their teacher and with the approval of their parent.

3. Secondary students may obtain an individual e-mail account with the approval of their parent.

5. [sic] You and your parent must sign an Account Agreement to be granted an individual e-mail account on * (system). This Agreement must be renewed on an annual basis. Your parent can withdraw their approval at any time.

6. If approved by your building principal, you may create a personal Web page on * (system). All material placed on your Web page must be preapproved in a manner specified by the school. Material placed on your Web page must relate to your school and career preparation activities.

## C. Unacceptable Uses

The following uses of * (system) are considered unacceptable:

### 1. Personal Safety

a. You will not post personal contact information about yourself or other people. Personal contact information includes your address, telephone, school address, work address, etc.

b. You will not agree to meet with someone you have met online without your parent's approval. Your parent should accompany you to this meeting.

c. You will promptly disclose to your teacher or other school employee any message you receive that is inappropriate or makes you feel uncomfortable.

### 2. Illegal Activities

a. You will not attempt to gain unauthorized access to * (system) or to any other computer system through * (system) or go beyond your authorized access. This includes attempting to log in through another person's account or access another person's files. These actions are illegal, even if only for the purposes of "browsing".

b. You will not make deliberate attempts to disrupt the computer system or destroy data by spreading computer viruses or by any other means. These actions are illegal.

c. You will not use * (system) to engage in any other illegal act, such as arranging for a drug sale or the purchase of alcohol, engaging in criminal gang activity, threatening the safety of person, etc.

### 3. System Security

a. You are responsible for your individual account and should take all reasonable precautions to prevent others from being able to use your account. Under no conditions should you provide your password to another person.

b. You will immediately notify a teacher or the system administrator if you have identified a possible security problem. Do not go looking for security problems, because this may be construed as an illegal attempt to gain access.

c. You will avoid the inadvertent spread of computer viruses by following the District virus protection procedures if you download software.

### 4. Inappropriate Language

a. Restrictions against Inappropriate Language apply to public messages, private messages, and material posted on Web pages.

b. You will not use obscene, profane, lewd, vulgar, rude, inflammatory, threatening, or disrespectful language.

c. You will not post information that could cause damage or a danger of disruption.

d. You will not engage in personal attacks, including prejudicial or discriminatory attacks.

e. You will not harass another person. Harassment is persistently acting in a manner that distresses or annoys another person. If you are told by a person to stop sending them messages, you must stop.

f. You will not knowingly or recklessly post false or defamatory information about a person or organization.

### 5. Respect for Privacy

a. You will not repost a message that was sent to you privately without permission of the person who sent you the message.

b. You will not post private information about another person.

### 6. Respecting Resource Limits.

a. You will use the system only for educational and career development activities and limited, high-quality, self-discovery activities. There is no limit on use for education and career development activities. The limit on self-discovery activities is no more than * (number) hours per week.

b. You will not download large files unless absolutely necessary. If necessary, you will download the file at a time when the system is not being heavily used and immediately remove the file from the system computer to your personal computer.

c. You will not post chain letters or engage in "spamming". Spamming is sending an annoying or unnecessary message to a large number of people.

d. You will check your e-mail frequently, delete unwanted messages promptly, and stay within your e-mail quota.

e. You will subscribe only to high quality discussion group mail lists that are relevant to your education or career development.

### 7. Plagiarism and Copyright Infringement

a. You will not plagiarize works that you find on the Internet. Plagiarism is taking the ideas or writings of others and presenting them as if they were yours.

b. You will respect the rights of copyright owners. Copyright infringement occurs when you inappropriately reproduce a work that is protected by a copyright. If a work contains language that specifies appropriate use of that work, you should follow the expressed requirements. If you are unsure whether or not you can use a work, you should request permission from the copyright owner. Copyright law can be very confusing. If you have questions ask a teacher.

### 8. Inappropriate Access to Material

a. You will not use * (system) to access material that is profane or obscene (pornography), that advocates illegal acts, or that advocates violence or discrimination towards other people (hate literature). A special exception may be made for hate literature if the purpose of your access is to conduct research and both your teacher and parent have approved.

b. If you mistakenly access inappropriate information, you should immediately tell your teacher or another District employee * (or disclose this access in the manner specified by your school). This will protect you against a claim that you have intentionally violated this Policy.

c. Your parents should instruct you if there is additional material that they think it would be inappropriate for you to access. The district fully expects that you will follow your parent's instructions in this matter.

## D. Your Rights

### 1. Free Speech

Your right to free speech, as set forth in the * (disciplinary code), applies also to your communication on the Internet. The * (system) is considered a limited forum, similar to the school newspaper, and therefore the District may restrict your speech for valid educational reasons. The District will not restrict your speech on the basis of a disagreement with the opinions you are expressing.

### 2. Search and Seizure

a. You should expect only limited privacy in the contents of your personal files on the District system. The situation is similar to the rights you have in the privacy of your locker.

b. Routine maintenance and monitoring of * (system) may lead to discovery that you have violated this Policy, the * (disciplinary code), or the law.

c. An individual search will be conducted if there is reasonable suspicion that you have violated this Policy, the * (disciplinary code), or the law. The investigation will be reasonable and related to the suspected violation.

d. Your parents have the right at any time to request to see the contents of your e-mail files.

### 3. Due Process

a. The District will cooperate fully with local, state, or federal officials in any investigation related to any illegal activities conducted through * (system).

b. In the event there is a claim that you have violated this Policy or * (disciplinary code) in your use of the * (system), you will be provided with a written notice of the suspected violation and an opportunity to present an explanation before a neutral administrator [or will be provided with notice and opportunity to be heard in the manner set forth in the * (disciplinary code)].

c. If the violation also involves a violation of other provisions of the * (disciplinary code), it will be handled in a manner described in the * (disciplinary code). Additional restrictions may be placed on your use of your Internet account.

## *E. Limitation of Liability*

The District makes no guarantee that the functions or the services provided by or through the District system will be error-free or without defect. The District will not be responsible for any damage you may suffer, including but not limited to, loss of data or interruptions of service. The District is not responsible for the accuracy or quality of the information obtained through or stored on the system. The District will not be responsible for financial obligations arising through the unauthorized use of the system.

## *F. Personal Responsibility*

When you are using the * (system), it may feel like you can more easily break a rule and not get caught. This is not really true because whenever you do something on a network you leave little "electronic footprints," so the odds of getting caught are really about same as they are in the real world.

# Student Account Agreement Template

## Student Section

Student Name: _____

Grade: _____

School: _____

I have read the District Acceptable Use Policy. I agree to follow the rules contained in this Policy.
I understand that if I violate the rules my account can be terminated and I may face other disciplinary measures.

Student Signature: _____ Date: _____

## Parent or Guardian Section

I have read the District Acceptable Use Policy. (If dial-up access is provided—I will supervise my child's use of the system when my child is accessing the system from home.)

I hereby release the district, its personnel, and any institutions with which it is affiliated, from any and all claims and damages of any nature arising from my child's use of, or inability to use, the District system, including, but not limited to, claims that may arise from the unauthorized use of the system to purchase products or services.

I will instruct my child regarding any restrictions against accessing material that are in addition to the restrictions set forth in the District Acceptable Use Policy. I will emphasize to my child the importance of following the rules for personal safety.

I give permission to issue an account for my child and certify that the information contained in this form is correct.

Parent Signature: _____ Date: _____

Parent Name: _____

Home Address: _____ Phone: _____

## This space reserved for System Administrator

Assigned User Name: _____

Assigned Temporary Password: _____

# KEEPING KIDS SAFE!

## Keeping Kids Safe in the World of Technology

This section is reprinted with permission from "Keeping Kids Safe in the World of Technology," an Internet hotlist created by Linda W. Uhrenholt in conjunction with Pacific Bell Education First.

## Introduction

Technology has changed the way students learn and access information. Students around the world can tap into the National Earthquake Information Service to see minute-by-minute earthquakes, a teacher can go to the San Francisco Giants Web site to access a math activity involving baseball, and administrators can interview job candidates across the globe via video conferencing. Technology makes for exciting times in education but what happens when "the dark side of technology" sneaks around a corner into the classroom?

The top three safety solutions in Keeping Kids Safe in the World of Technology are EDUCATION, SUPERVISION, and SOFTWARE. Using the links listed here, explore some of these possible solutions. This represents a very small portion of Internet sites recognizing the importance of this topic.

## The Internet Resources

### Online Safety Guides

- FBI Internet Safety Tips! (http://www.fbi.gov/kids/kids.htm). Federal Bureau of Investigation Kids & Youth Educational Page. This includes information on Internet safety tips, law enforcement stories, and crime detection.

- What You Should Know as a Parent (http://www.yahooligans.com/docs/safety/parents.html). The Yahooligans perspective on how parents can reduce online risks associated with technology. Presented by Yahoo search directory authors of Yahooligans, an Internet search guide for kids.

- National Center for Missing and Exploited Children (http://www.missingkids.com). Child Safety on the Information Highway is a wonderful brochure that can be ordered from this organization. Think about mailing this out in a school newsletter or distributing at your School Technology Night.

- A Family Friendly Internet (http://www.whitehouse.gov/WH/New/Ratings). The White House strategy on keeping the Internet a "family friendly" place.

- Netparents.org (http://www.netparents.org). This site is dedicated to providing information and resources to parents about the Internet and the use of other technologies.

- Enough Is Enough (http://www.enough.org). An organization that provides extensive information on how to take action against hard-core pornography on the Internet. Included are myths and legends, blocking software, kid safe sites, and acceptable use policies.

- CyberAngels (http://www.cyberangels.org). The primary goal of this organization is to educate Internet users in safety awareness while online. This Internet safety organization was founded by members of The International Alliance of Guardian Angels.

- Electronic Crime Branch of the United States Secret Service (http://www.treas.gov/usss/investigation/investigate-info.html). Discussions of what the Secret Service does in terms of computer crimes, including threats to the President.

- Computer Incident Advisory Capability (CIAC) (http://ciac.llnl.gov/ciac/CIACHoaxes.html). Department of Energy site designed to expose Internet hoaxes.

- California State Department of Education (http://goldmine.cde.ca.gov). Teaching, Learning and Technology is the California State Department of Education's technology overview.

- Pacific Bell Education First Knowledge Network Explorer (http://www.kn.pacbell.com). This is an award-winning site for education. Safe online activities are presented as well as information regarding technology use in education and libraries.

## *Libraries and the Internet*

- Librarians Guide to Cyberspace for Parents and Kids (http://www.ssdesign. com/parentspage/greatsites). This site is brought online by the American Library Association and covers such things as safety tips and help for parents interested in technology.

- ALA Resolution on Filtering Software in Libraries (http://www.ala.org/ alaorg/oif/filt_res.html). American Library Council's statement on the use of filtering and blocking software in libraries.

- Around the Web in 80 Minutes (http://www.kn.pacbell.com/wired/Round Web/index.html). Designed to give librarians an overview of the World Wide Web. Included are sites called "library hotspots" for accessing information on acceptable use policies, filtering, and other current library issues.

## *Filtering, Blocking, and Monitoring Software*

- Junk Mail Removal (http://dir.yahoo.com/Business_and_Economy/ Companies/Computers/Communications_and_Networking/Software/Elect ronic_Mail/Junk_Email_Removal/). The Web directory Yahoo's listing of junk mail removal programs.

- URLabs/I-Gear (http://www.urlabs.com/public/). More than an Internet filter! Provides customized access permission, dynamic document reviews, and simple addition and deletion of existing entries.

- CyperPatrol (http://www.cyberpatrol.com/). Filtering software that blocks objectionable sex sites. Can set the time of day for access.

- Cyber Sitter (http://www.solidoak.com/cysitter.htm). Access software that blocks offensive sites. Blocks URLs but not IP addresses at this time. Can alert parents via e-mail when violations occur.

- Cyber Snoop (http://www.pearlsw.com). Filters out inappropriate sites, shuts down connection when this occurs. Can display content of a chat session.

- Net Nanny (http://www.netnanny.com). Filtering software that allows for addition of objectionable sites. Can stop names and addresses.

- Internet Watch Dog (http://www.charlesriver.com/titles/watchdog.html). Software that can capture screen shots of computer activity is provided here. It generates a report that lists sites visited by a user.

- Surf Watch (http://www.surfwatch.com). The software discussed here blocks sites and terms. Users can add sites to the database and can test a site to see if it is blocked and, if so the reason why it is blocked.

## Search Engines for Kids and Off-Line Solutions

- Yahooligans! (http://www.yahooligans.com). A Web guide for kids 8-14 years of age.

- Magellan (http://www.mckinley.com). A search engine that allows kids to search for information in "green light" sites (for students under 15 years of age).

- Web Buddy (http://www.dataviz.com). Software designed to download an entire Web site for off-line browsingis available here. Students can still discover the World Wide Web in a controlled atmosphere.

- WebWhacker (http://www.bluesquirrel.com). This software program allows users to download entire sites including text and graphics to disk or hard drive for off-line usage which can be especially helpful in elementary grades or when your school is not connected.

## Videoconferencing for Learning

- Videoconferencing for Learning (http://www.kn.pacbell.com/vidconf). Part of Pacific Bell Education First Web site, this area explains the technology involved in videoconferencing as well as usage and etiquette.

- Distance Learning Resource Network (http://www.wested.org/tie/dlrn/). The organization is a nonprofit association used to promote the application of distance learning for education and training.

# Getting Connected

## INTERNET CONNECTION

Computers at different locations can communicate with each other over networks that are connected by high-speed telephone lines. Information or data is sent over these networks in the form of electronic signals. In order to make a basic connection, the following hardware is needed: computer workstation, printer, and a modem or network card—most often an Ethernet adapter. Full Internet access, including the World Wide Web, e-mail, FTP (File Transfer Protocol), telnet, and other useful tools, can be obtained in a variety of ways: PPP dial-up access over existing copper wire, cable, ISDN, ADSL, or LAN/ WAN. You will also need Internet client software programs.

PPP dial-up is simply using a modem, telephone line, and local phone number to directly connect to the Internet through an Internet Service Provider. A cable connection uses coaxial cable, an Ethernet adapter card, and a specially designed cable modem to connect directly to the Internet. Direct connections through a LAN or WAN require a network card and a high-speed line such as 56K or T1. You must also be running TCP/IP (Transmission Control Protocol/ Internet Protocol) on your workstation. This allows data to be transferred between the networks using the same protocol or language. TCP/IP was developed as the standard because data must travel over many different operating systems. The computer workstation on your desktop is considered the client. The computer you are connected with is considered the host or server.

Many schools and most universities have high-speed line connections to the Internet. Contact the system operator to see if there is a way to gain connection

through their computer network. State networks, free-nets, and public library networks are other options. Local and national Internet Service Providers provide home accounts for a monthly fee.

## America Online

America Online provides Internet access while allowing you to explore information provided on its own network. AOL also provides you with proprietary software for connecting to its service. It is a graphical interface that is user-friendly and easy to navigate. To connect to America Online, you need a computer workstation, 28.8 kbps modem or higher, standard telephone line, AOL software, and a credit card for registering directly online. The software is free with an initial number of free hours.

## Dial-Up PPP

In this configuration you need a computer workstation, modem, standard telephone line, an Internet service provider that allows a PPP (Point to Point Protocol)

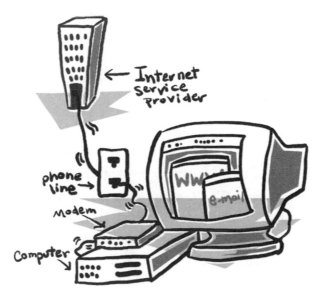

connection, and Internet client software for the World Wide Web, e-mail, FTP, and telnet. Many universities and Internet Service Providers provide this type of dial-up connection and software package. You must be running TCP/IP and PPP software. The faster the modem the better. A 33.6 kbps modem is adequate for e-mail and some Web browsing. However, if you want to download large files or access multimedia-intensive World Wide Web pages, you should have a 56 kbps modem or higher.

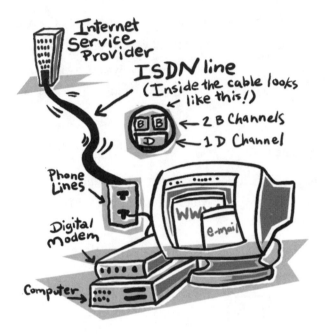

## ISDN

ISDN (Integrated Systems Digital Network) is a digital rather than traditional analog telephone line. It consists of two 64 kbps channels called B channels and one D or delta channel. The B channels are used for voice or data. The D channel is used for signaling or x.25 packet networking. It is not available in all areas. In order to use this setup, you must have an ISDN line installed, a computer workstation, terminal adapter, also called a digital modem, and a PPP account. You must be running TCP/IP and PPP software on your workstation.

You can run a full range of Internet client software, including e-mail, Web browsers, FTP, and telnet.

## LAN/WAN

In this option, you must be connected to a local area network (LAN) or Wide Area Network (WAN) that provides a link to the Internet via a router. You must have TCP/IP running on your workstation along with a network card. With this configuration you can run graphical user interface programs for the World Wide Web, e-mail, FTP, and telnet. Files are transferred very quickly. Some video and audio capabilities are also possible with programs such as CUSeeMe (videoconferencing) and RealPlayer. You will need a workstation with at least 100 MHz processing speed and a video or digital camera. If you want to view video at thirty frames per second, you need an even faster connection such as a fiber ATM (Asynchronous Transfer Mode) and a huge amount of RAM and disk storage space.

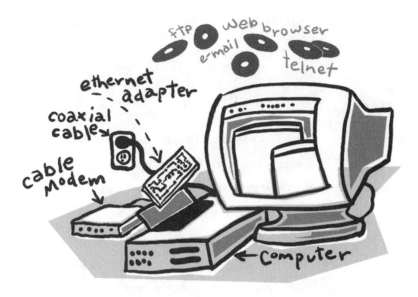

## Cable Modem

In some areas of the country, a cable modem is the best option for high-speed connectivity. Existing coaxial cable lines form the backbone to deliver a digital network system. You will need a computer workstation, a cable modem, and an ethernet adapter. TCP/IP needs to be configured for the network. Software for connecting to the network will be provided by the cable company. You can run all of your Internet client software, including Web browsers, e-mail, FTP, and telnet.

# FUTURE OPTIONS

## ADSL

Asymmetric Digital Subscriber Service is poised to enter the telecommunications market. This technology uses existing copper wire and separates the line into segments that can be utilized at the same time. The drawback to this connection option is that beyond a 3.5 mile range of the telephone switching station, the quality drops off. This is probably not a choice for rural areas.

## MMDS

Multichannel Multipoint Distribution Service is a wireless system that uses microwave frequencies to provide high-speed downloads. An analog modem can be used with this service along with an antenna installed at your site.

# INTERNET CLIENT SOFTWARE PROGRAMS

When choosing a connection option that links you to the Internet, you need client software programs to run on your computer workstation. This software allows you to e-mail, browse the Web, transfer files, and access other computer terminals. E-mail and newsreaders are part of the Netscape and Internet Explorer programs. However, you may wish to have a separate e-mail program.

Many Internet programs are available individually as freeware or shareware from a variety of Web sites or from commercial providers such as America Online. Some Internet Service Providers, universities, and schools package a set of programs already configured for connecting to their systems. This takes the sting out of setting up connection configurations with little or no documentation.

# Shareware and Freeware

If you are adventurous or frugal, here are some shareware (small fee to developer) and freeware (free) programs with Web sites listed on which to obtain them.

## *Windows*

### Browser:

Netscape Navigator
(http://home.netscape.com)

Internet Explorer
(http://www.microsoft.com)

### Compression:

WinZip
(http://www.winzip.com/)

### E-Mail:

Eudora Lite
(http://www.eudora.com)

### FTP:

WS_FTP
(http://www.ipswitch.com/downloads/ws_ftp_LE.html)

### News Streaming:

Educast
(http://www.educast.com)

### Teleconferencing:

CUSeeMe (videoconferencing)—Freeware Version
(ftp://gated.cornell.edu/pub/cu-seeme/html/Welcome.html)

CUSeeMe—White Pine Software
(http://www.wpine.com/Products/CU-SeeMe/)

Microsoft NetMeeting

(http://www.microsoft.com/netmeeting/)

## Telnet:

Windows 95 has telnet built into the operating system. You can find it in the Windows folder. Make a shortcut or add it to your Start Menu.

## *Macintosh*

## Browser:

Netscape Navigator

(http://home.netscape.com)

Internet Explorer

(http://www.microsoft.com)

## Compression:

Stuffit Expander (http://www.aladdinsys.com/expander/expander1.html)

## E-mail:

Eudora

(http://www.eudora.com)

## FTP:

Anarchie

(http://www.stairways.com/anarchie/index.html)

Fetch

(http://www.dartmouth.edu/pages/softdev/fetch.html)

## News Streaming:

Educast

(http://www.educast.com)

## Teleconferencing:

CUSeeMe (videoconferencing)—Freeware Version

(ftp://gated.cornell.edu/pub/cu-seeme/html/Welcome.html)

CUSeeMe—White Pine Software
(http://www.wpine.com/Products/CU-SeeMe/)

Timbuktu Pro
(http://www.netopia.com/software/tb2/mac/)

**Telnet:**

NCSA Telnet
(http://www.ncsa.uiuc.edu/SDG/Software/)

# Plug-Ins

In order to enjoy some of the multimedia offerings on the Web, you will need software programs called plug-ins. These are free from software developers and designed for both the Macintosh and Windows operating systems. You install them into the

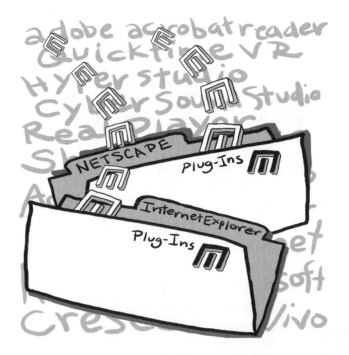

plug-in folder of Netscape or Internet Explorer. If you want advanced features of these plug-ins, you will need to purchase the commercial version. Below is a list of the most popular plug-ins that run on both Macintosh and Windows operating systems. You will also want to read the system specifications before downloading the programs. Some of them require certain processors and high-speed connections to the Internet in order for them to run properly.

- Adobe Acrobat Reader (http://www.adobe.com/prodindex.acrobat/read step.html). Portable Document Files (PDF) made with Adobe Acrobat can be read within the browser using Adobe Acrobat Reader. You cannot create PDF files with Adobe Acrobat Reader.

- Crescendo (http://www.liveupdate.com). Digital music made with a keyboard are saved as midi files on the Web. Crescendo and QuickTime allow you to hear the music as soon as you hit the page. Midi files are popular because they can be compressed to very small files, thus taking very little bandwidth on the Internet. The plug-ins, Crescendo and Live Audio, allow you to listen to these files.

- CakeWalk Home Studio (http://cakewalk.com/). This sound program for Windows enables users to record and edit sound with instruments, vocals, or the Virtual Piano. Additionally, scrolling lyrics may be incorporated during record and playback.

- CyberSound Studio for Macintosh (http://www.cybersound.com). This is an inexpensive program to get started using midi. It comes with a keyboard and software with many musical instruments. In fact, you can use the program without the keyboard to create midi files.

- HyperStudio (http://www.hyperstudio.com/index.shtml). HyperStudio is a multimedia authoring program that allows you to incorporate sounds, pictures, movies, and text into a hyperlinked sequence. The plug-in gives you the ability to view hyperstudio stacks within the browser.

- QuickTime (http://www.apple.com/quicktime/). View videoclips in the browser.

- QuickTime VR (http://quicktime.apple.com). QuickTime Virtual Reality allows the viewer to rotate a picture from different angles and to zoom in and out. Some QTVR movies are 180 or 360 panoramic views.

- RealPlayer (http://www.real.com). RealAudio is audio streaming over the Internet in real time. This means you can listen to live radio broadcasts in other parts of the world or large prerecorded files without waiting for them to download. All you need is the RealPlayer plug-in, which is free. If you want to create RealAudio files for your own home page, your server must be running the RealAudio server software from Real Networks. If your Internet Service Provider already has the software, you won't need to purchase it. In addition, you may want to buy a commercial version of the player, which has preset buttons so you can go directly to your favorite stations on the Web. The technology has now reached a point where the RealPlayer software also allows video streaming.

- Shockwave (http://www.macromedia.com). Interactive multimedia modules are created with Macromedia's Shockwave. It's like having a CD-ROM on the Web.

- VivoActive Player (http://www.vivo.com). The Vivo plug-in allows you to play videos, but doesn't allow you to save them for future viewing.

# SETTING UP A PPP CONNECTION—WINDOWS 95

## Configuring the "Network" Control Panel

The "Network" Control Panel controls the way your computer accesses a network (i.e., using a Network card or Dial-Up Adapter—more commonly referred to as a modem). Follow the setup instructions that follow according to your connection method. (Note: You may need to have your Windows 95 Setup Disks or CD-ROM available.)

1. Open the "Control Panel," then open the "Network" item. You will see a window as shown in Figure A.1. Make sure the following Network Components have been added. If they have not been added, add them and remove any unnecessary components (Note: If your computer is NOT connected to a LAN (Local Area Network), then these three components are the only ones you will need.)

   • Client for Microsoft Networks (Client, Microsoft)

   • Dial-Up Adapter (Adapter, Microsoft)

   • TCP/IP (Protocol, Microsoft).

2. The "Primary Network Logon" should be set to "Windows Logon." Next, click on the "Identification" tab and enter a name and workgroup for your computer. (Note: The name should be one word.)

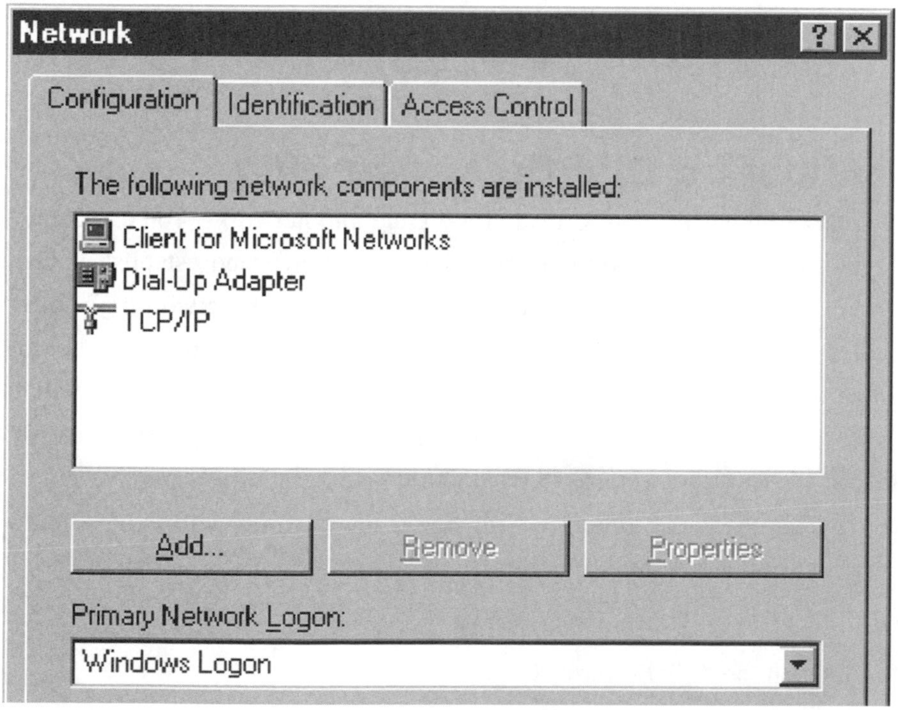

**FIGURE A.1**

3. Click on "TCP/IP" and then select "Properties." You will see a window as shown in Figure A.2. Next, select the following tabs and ensure that the settings match appropriately:

- IP Address: Obtain IP Address Automatically

- WinsConfiguration: Disable WINS Resolution

- DNS Configuration: Disable DNS

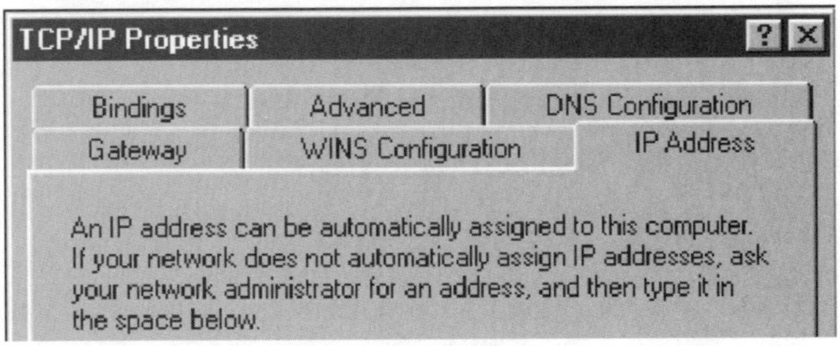

*FIGURE A.2*

4. Select "OK" for each window until you exit from the "Network" control panel. You may be told to restart your computer.

# Configuring Dial-Up Networking

Windows 95 has its own software for dialing into networks. You can configure this software to dial into your Internet Service Provider and establish your PPP session. To find out if your computer has the "Dial-Up Networking" software installed, double click on the "My Computer" icon on the desktop. You should see a folder named "Dial-Up Networking." If you do not see the folder, you will have to install the software. Follow the steps below.(Note: You may need to have your Windows 95 Setup Disks or CD-ROM available.)

1. Open the "My Computer" icon on the desktop. You will see a window as shown in Figure A.3.

2. Open the "Control Panel" folder.

3. Open the "Add/Remove Programs" icon.

4. In the new window, click on the "Windows Setup" tab.

**FIGURE A.3**

5. Double click on the "Communications" item so a new window appears listing which components are currently installed.

6. Click the check-box next to "Dial-Up Networking" so that a check appears.

7. Click on the "Okay" button.

8. When you are back at the "Add/Remove Programs" window, you can click on the "Okay" button.

After the installation process, you will want to restart your computer for Windows 95 to update and display the folder in "My Computer."

# Creating a Connection to Your Internet Service Provider

You can follow the steps below to create a connection to your Internet Service Provider.

1. When you are back at the desktop, open the "My Computer" folder and then open the "Dial-Up Networking" folder. You will see a window as shown in Figure A.4 on the next page.

2. If you have a connection already created for your Internet Service Provider, click the right mouse button and then select the "Properties" item from the drop down list; otherwise you will first have to "Make New Connection." The name can be your Internet Service Provider. The phone number is the 10 digits you use to dial-up and connect.

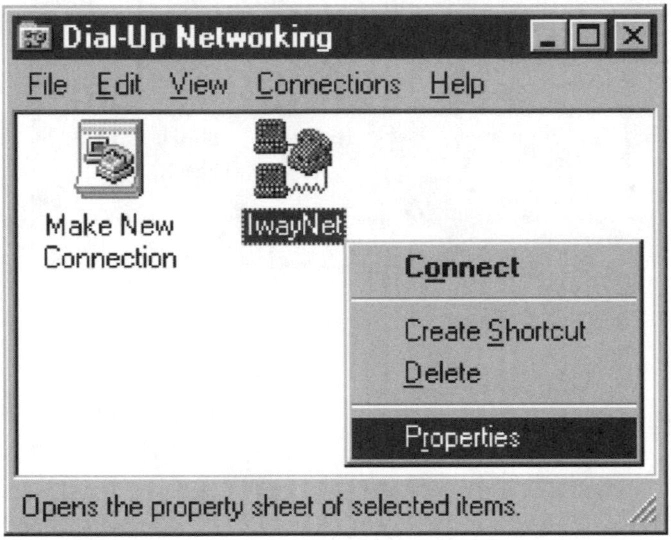

*FIGURE A.4*

3. Near the bottom of the "Properties"window you will see a button named "Server Type," select it. You will see a window as shown in Figure A.5.

4. You should see "Type of Dial-Up Server" and it should read "PPP: Windows 95, Windows NT 3.5, Internet."

5. Under the "Advanced options" section, only "Enable software compression" should be checked.

6. Under the "Allowed network protocols" section, only "TCP/IP" should be checked.

7. Click on the button "TCP/IP Settings."
   a. "Server assigned IP address" should be marked.

b. "Specify name server addresses" should be marked.

    i. "Primary DNS" is a series of numbers provided by your ISP.

    ii. "Secondary DNS" is a series of numbers provided by your ISP.

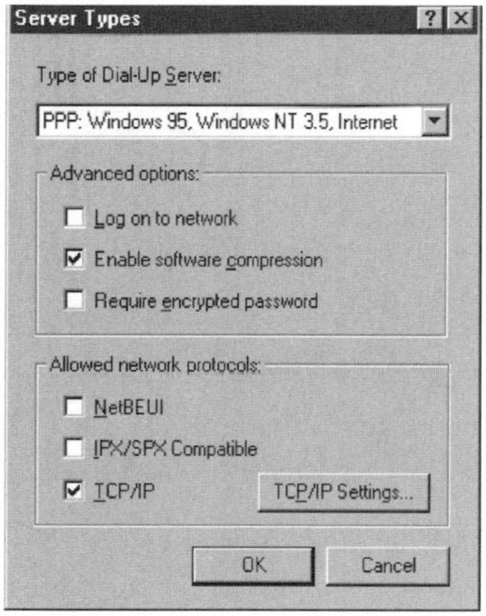

*FIGURE A.5*

Click on every "OK" button (as shown in Figure A.6) until you are back at the desktop with the "Dial-Up Networking" folder open. You are done configuring your ISP connection.

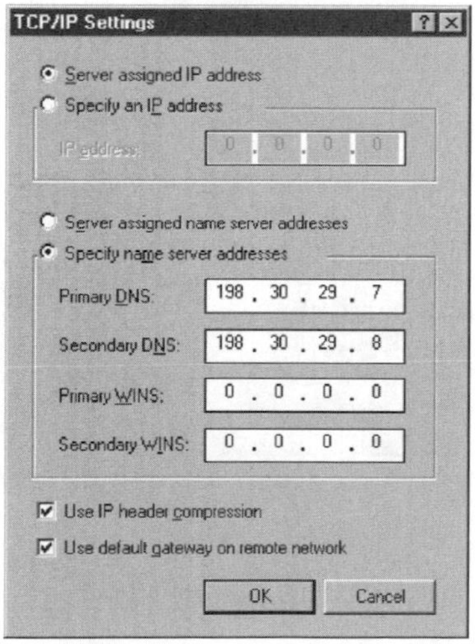

*FIGURE A.6*

## Logging On to the Internet

To connect to the Internet, open the "My Computer" icon on the desktop and then open the "Dial-Up Networking" folder. Double click on the icon you created for your ISP. Type in your User Name in the "User Name" field and your Password in the "Password" field.

Click on the "Connect" button to connect to the service. You should see a new dialog window that informs you of the status of the connection. When you see "Connected" and a timer counting the seconds you have been online, you may "minimize" the connection window and begin to use your Internet applications.

# SETTING UP A PPP CONNECTION–MACINTOSH

1. From the "Apple" menu, select "Control Panels" then "PPP" (see Figure A.7).

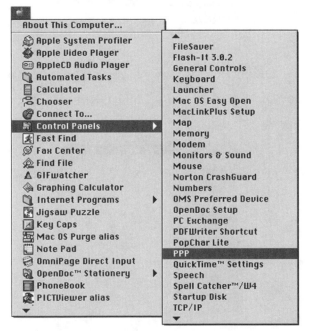

**FIGURE A.7**

2. You will see a window as shown in Figure A.8.  Type in your name.

3. Type in your password.

4. Check the "Save Password" box.

5. Type in the number for connecting to your Internet Service Provider.

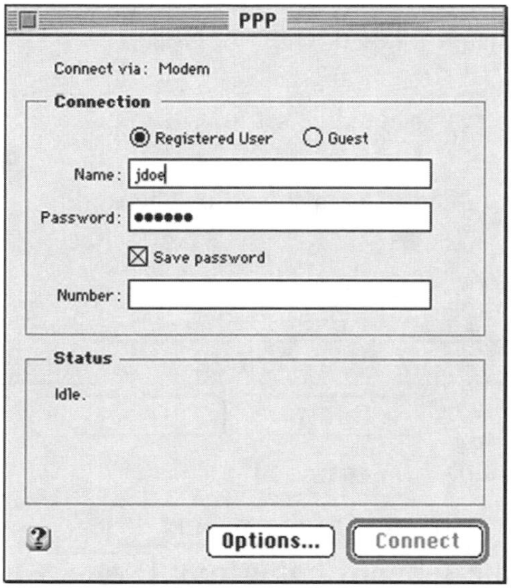

**FIGURE A.8**

## Setting Up the Modem

1. From the PPP menu, select "Modem."

2. Choose which port your modem is using.

3. Under Setup, select your modem type.

4. Check "Sound On."

5. Check tone.

## ConfigPPP Setup

The ConfigPPP is another program used to connect a Macintosh to the Internet. Depending on which version of ConfigPPP you have, the accompanying screen shots (see Figures A.9 - A.11) may or may not be identical to your actual windows.

1. From the "Apple" menu select the "Control Panels" option and then "ConfigPPP." You will see a window as shown in Figure A.9.

2. The "Port Name" should be set to: Modem Port.

3. The "Idle Time out" should be set to: None.

4. The "Echo Interval" should be set to: Off.

5. The "Hangup on Close" item should be checked.

6. The "Quiet Mode" item should be checked.

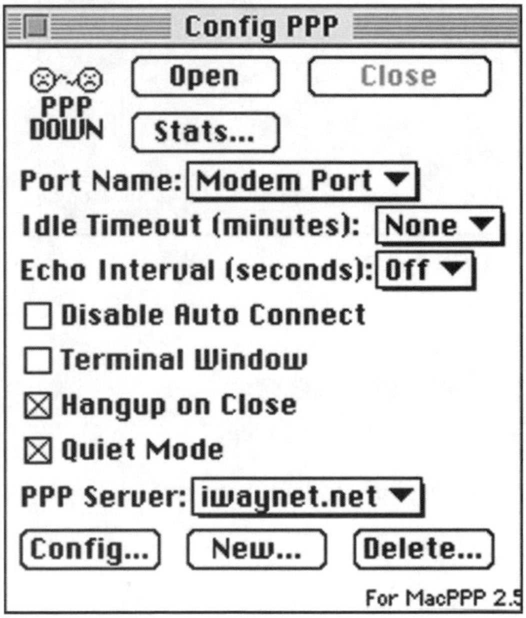

**FIGURE A.9**

7. Select the "Config" button. You will see a window as shown in Figure A.10.

8. In the "PPP Server Name" box, type in the domain name of your ISP (example: iwaynet.net).

9. The "Port Speed" should be set as follows: If you have a 28.8 modem try using 57600, if you have a 14.4 modem try using 38400.

10. The "Flow Control" should be set to: CTS & RTS (DTR). Note: If you experience problems connecting, you can try changing this option to "None."

11. Select either "Tone Dial" or "Pulse Dial" for the dialing type.

12. In the "Phone num" box, type in your ISP's access number (add any necessary prefixes if you need them, i.e., 9).

13. In the "Modem Init" box, type in the proper modem initialization string (i.e., AT&F1).

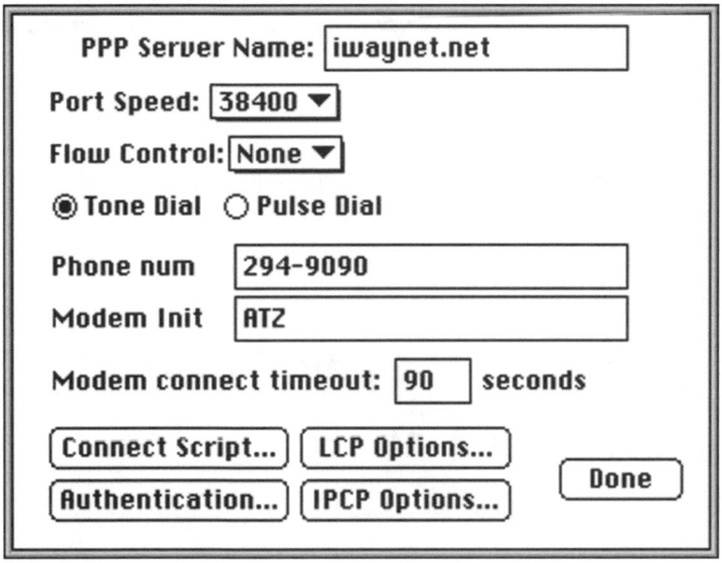

```
┌─────────────────────────────────────────────┐
│  PPP Server Name: │iwaynet.net          │     │
│  Port Speed: │38400 ▼│                         │
│  Flow Control:│None ▼│                          │
│  ◉ Tone Dial  ○ Pulse Dial                     │
│  Phone num    │294-9090              │          │
│  Modem Init   │ATZ                   │          │
│  Modem connect timeout: │90  │ seconds          │
│  [ Connect Script... ] [ LCP Options... ]       │
│  [ Authentication... ] [ IPCP Options... ] [ Done ] │
└─────────────────────────────────────────────┘
```

**FIGURE A.10**

14. Click on the "Authentication …" button. You will see a window as shown in Figure A.11 on the next page.

15. In the "Auth. ID" box, type in your USERNAME (It is case sensitive).

16. In the "Password" box, type in your PASSWORD (It is case sensitive).

17. Click on the "OK" button.

18. Click on the "Done" button.

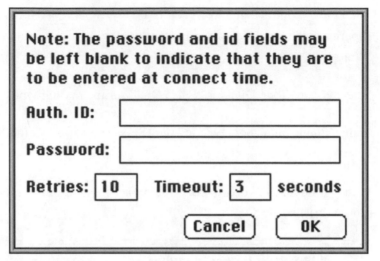

Note: The password and id fields may be left blank to indicate that they are to be entered at connect time.

Auth. ID: [                    ]

Password: [                    ]

Retries: [10]    Timeout: [3]    seconds

[ Cancel ]    [ OK ]

FIGURE A.11

You are done with the configuration process. Click on the "Open" button to connect.

# Setting Up TCP/IP Open Transport (System 7.5.2 and Above)

The following settings are for the TCP/IP Control Panel. You must have a PPP client (i.e., MacPPP, FreePPP, or PPP) installed to follow the setup process. PPP comes with Mac OS System 7.6 and higher.

1. From the "Apple" menu, select "Control Panels" and then "TCP/IP." You will see a window as shown in Figure A.12.

2. For the "Connect Via" option, select the PPP Client that is present on your system (i.e., MacPPP, FreePPP, or PPP).

3. For the "Configure" option, select "Using PPP Server."

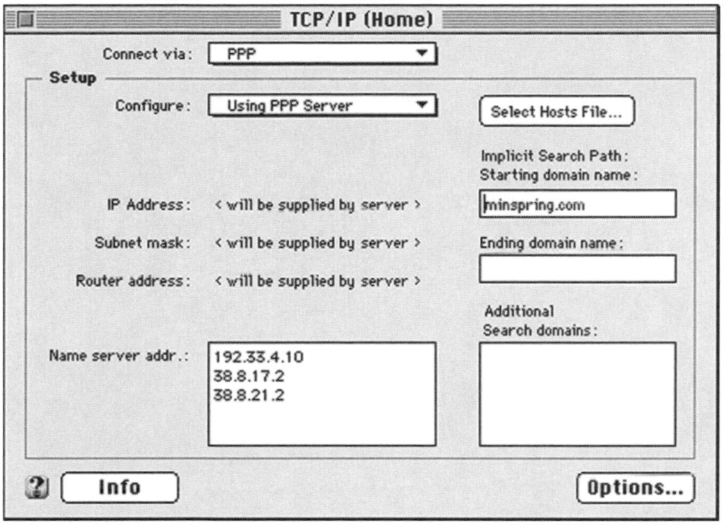

**FIGURE A.12**

4. Under "Implicit Search Path" for the "Starting domain name" box, type in the domain name of your Internet Service Provider (example: mind spring.com).

5. For the "Name server addr." box, type in the string of numbers given to you by your ISP.

# Logging On to the Internet

1. From the Apple Menu select "PPP" or "ConfigPPP."

2. Click on "Connect."

# Accessing Information

## E-MAIL

Electronic mail allows you to communicate with others over a network. The advantages of e-mail are instant correspondence with colleagues, access to listserv discussion groups, and a presence in the global community.

There are many "whois" directories or white pages for finding a person's e-mail address. Your Internet Service Provider may provide a directory of the people with accounts on its system, and, generally, you can search for a person by typing in his or her name. Other systems provide a directory that is more globally oriented. There is no one directory that lists all the people on the Internet.

Many different types of e-mail programs allow you to communicate over the Internet. The basic information you must know is the address of the person for correspondence and a few commands. Internet addresses are expressed in terms of the userid (user identification) at the place where the person has an account called the domain or host. Here is an example of an e-mail address:

userid@domain (also called host)

jdoe@osu.edu

In this example, the host is edu. It tells you that this is an educational institution. You can also identify the geographical location of hosts such as the United States by the extension "us." The most common domains are shown here:

.com    commercial

.edu    education

.gov    government

.mil    military

.net    network

.org    organization

# Sending an E-Mail Message

In the To: line, type the person's e-mail address. In the subject line type what your message is about. You can send a carbon copy or blind carbon copy to another individual by typing their e-mail address in the CC: or the BCC: line. Type your message in the message box. After composing your e-mail, click on the send button.

To:        jdoe@hotmail.com

Subject:   topic for discussion

Cc:        address of a secondary person or persons whom you want to receive the message

Bcc:       address of a secondary person or persons whom you want to receive the message wihtout the knowledge of the primary recipient.

Type your message in the designated area.

On the Internet, you will find several Web-based e-mail programs. When you join one of these services for free, there may be advertising sent to your e-mail address. However, they are popular among people who do not have any direct Internet access through a service provider. Below is a partial listing.

Hot Mail (see Figure B.1)
(http://www.hotmail.com)

Rocket Mail (see Figure B.2)
(http://www.rocketmail.com)

If all you need is a free e-mail service with a local access number, try Juno mail (http://www.juno.com) (see Figure B.3 on page 136). It uses proprietary software to connect you to its service.

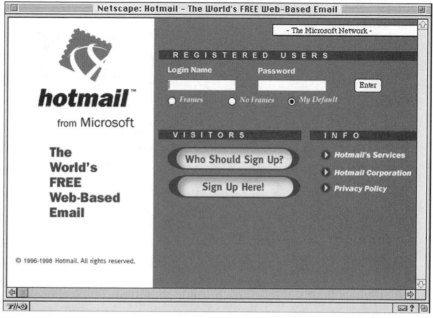

**FIGURE B.1**

**FIGURE B.2**

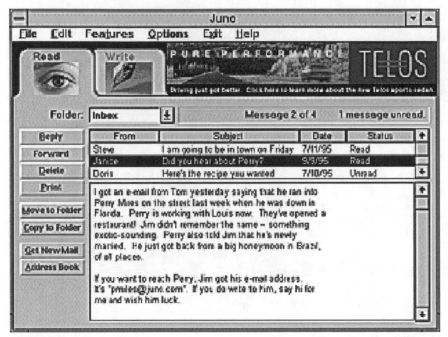

**FIGURE B.3**

**FIGURE B.4**

If you want to check your e-mail using the Web, try Mailstart (http://www.mailstart.com) (see Figure B.4).

# Signature File

A signature file is one you create that will automatically be appended to your e-mail. Your signature is information unique to you. Generally, it will have your name, address of your organization, a phone number, and your e-mail or Web address. Some signatures contain a quote or witticism. The established netiquette is that the signature be no longer than four lines. Most e-mail programs have a menu area where you can create and save your signature file.

Example of a signature file:

| | |
|---|---|
| Jane C. Doe | Somewhere Public Schools |
| Library Media Specialist | Main Street |
| xxx-xxx-xxxx | Anytown, Ohio 43211 |
| jdoe@osu.edu | |

# Attachments

You can share documents and photographs via e-mail by sending them as attached files. Since each e-mail program differs in the way it handles attachments (some have no provision for them at all), you should read the instructions.

## Smiles, Smilies, or Smileys

When communicating on the Internet, your facial expressions and vocal intonations are not visible or audible. You might say something you think is funny, but the person on the receiving end may not understand. This is where smiles come into play. Smiles are typed character patterns on the screen that help the reader understand the meaning of what you are saying. There are some basic designs as well as more elaborate ones and they are fun to create. In fact, there are smile dictionaries available on the Internet. The *Unofficial Smilie Dictionary* by Guy Kawasaki is one example.

Here are the basics from the *Unofficial Smilie Dictionary*:

:-)   Your basic smilie. This smilie is used to inflect a sarcastic or joking statement since we can't hear voice inflection over UNIX.

;-)   Winky smilie. User just made a flirtatious and/or sarcastic remark. More of a "don't hit me for what I just said" smilie.

:-(   Frowning smilie. User did not like that last statement or is upset or depressed about something.

:-I   Indifferent smilie. This is better than a Frowning smilie but not quite as good as a happy smilie

:->   User just made a really biting sarcastic remark. Worse than a :-).

>:->   User just made a really devilish remark.

>;->   Winky and devil combined. A very lewd remark was just made.

# ELECTRONIC DISCUSSION GROUPS

Electronic discussion groups, which are commonly referred to as "listservs" because Listserv is a prominent brand name of the software used for this purpose, are online discussion groups made up of people interested in specific topics. In order to participate in a discussion group, you must subscribe to the specific group. Subscription is free. Subscribing simply means you sign up to receive messages via e-mail. Hundreds of people subscribe to these groups and the messages can accumulate quickly. You will need to read your mail frequently to keep up with the postings. There are several places on the Web to locate electronic discussion groups.

• Directory of Scholarly and Professional E-Conferences
    (http://n2h2.com/KOVACS/)

• E-Mail Discussion Groups
    (http://alabanza.com/kabacoff/Inter-Links/listserv.html)

• List of Lists
    (http://catalog.com/vivian/interest-group-search.html)

• Listz, the mailing list directory
  (http://www.liszt.com/)

# Joining a Listserv Electronic Discussion Group

Here are listserv subscription step-by-step instructions:

Step 1.    Launch or connect to your e-mail program.

Step 2.    To: listserv@host (type in the listserv address)

Step 3.    Subject: (leave the subject blank)

Step 4.    CC: (leave blank)

Step 5.    In the body of the message type: subscribe listname your name

Step 6.    Send the message

> *Example:*
> To: listserv@listserv.syr.edu
> Subject: (leave blank)
> CC: (leave blank)
>
> _____
>
> subscribe lm_net jane doe

# Posting a Message

Once you are a discussion group subscriber, you will want to post messages for others in the discussion group to read. To post a message that will go to all subscribers, send an e-mail message to the discussion group, not the server.

> *Example:*
> To: lm_net@listserv.syr.edu
>
> Subject: (this can be the subject of the message you are sending)
>
> Cc:

---

Type your message

Send the message.

To reply to a message that all subscribers will read, simply click on the reply button, then type your message. To reply only to the individual, look for the person's Internet address in the message and send e-mail directly to them.

## Leaving a Listserv Discussion Group

To leave a discussion group, the method is similar to subscribing except that you replace subscribe with signoff or unsubscribe, whichever was specified in the instructions that you received after subscribing. Be sure to print and save the instructions for future reference.

*Example:*

To: listserv@listserv.syr.edu

Subject: (leave blank)

Cc: (leave blank)

---

signoff lm_net

### Special Notes

Remember that all e-mail sent to a listserv is going to a computer. There is no person to contact in the event a message bounces back. You cannot include a signature file when subscribing to a listserv.

# NEWSGROUPS

Networks provide literally thousands of discussion groups that can be read using the newsreader in your Web browser. The newsgroups are organized into seven Usenet groups: comp, news, rec, sci, soc, talk, and misc. There are other newsgroups that are similar to Usenet, but they have different names. These are alt, bionet, bit, biz, de, fi, ieee, gnu, k12, u3b, and vmsnet. There is also Clarinet, which is an indexed system of United Press International (UPI) and syndicated columns. This service is limited to organizations that contract for the service.

---

## K12NET NEWSGROUPS
### Conference Areas Available in K12Net

| Usenet Newsgroup | Description |
| --- | --- |
| k12.lang.francais | French Conversation |
| k12.lang.esp-eng | Spanish Conversation |
| k12.lang.deutsch-eng | German Conversation |
| k12.lang.russian | Russian Conversation |
| k12.lang.art | Language Arts Education |
| k12.ed.tag | Talented and Gifted |
| k12.ed.art | Art Education |
| k12.ed.music | Music Education |
| k12.ed.business | Business Education |
| k12.ed.health-pe | Health & Physical Education |
| k12.ed.life-skills | School Counselors |
| k12.ed.soc-studies | Social Studies Education |
| k12.ed.tech | Technical/Vocational Education |
| k12.ed.science | Science Education |
| k12.ed.math | Math Education |
| k12.ed.comp.literacy | Computer Literacy |
| k12.ed.special | Special Education |
| k12.chat.teacher | Teacher Chat |
| k12.library | Technology in Libraries |

---

# WORLD WIDE WEB

The World Wide Web is based on Hypertext Markup Language (HTML) that allows the user to jump from place to place through links. You navigate through these links using either a text or graphical browser. With a text browser, you highlight text and use your arrow keys. With a graphical browser, you use a mouse to point and click on highlighted text or icons.

The World Wide Web includes links to hypertext media, FTP, telnet, Usenet newsgroups, and other documents. A World Wide Web address on the Internet is called a URL (Uniform Resource Locator).

*URL examples:*

> ftp://rtfm.mit.edu

> http://www.enc.org

FTP (file transfer protocol) and http (hypertext transfer protocol) tell you the access method. The information after the colon tells you the address and directory path. It is important to know URLs when you want to go manually to a site.

Home pages are created by information providers or individuals as starting points to their resources using HTML. People in charge of a Web site are called Webmasters. For more information about the Web, read World Wide Web Frequently Asked Questions available via FTP at rtfm.mit.edu/pub/usenet/znews.answers/www/ or from Usenet newsgroups under news.answers.

If you would like to set up a Web server in your classroom, read the Classroom Internet Server Cookbook by Stephen E. Collins, which is available at http://web66.coled.umn.edu/Cookbook/.

# TELNET

Telnet allows you to log on to a remote host and interact as though you were actually sitting at that computer terminal. It is text based so there is no graphical interface. You might want to use telnet to access a local freenet or online catalog of library books.

To telnet through your Web browser, in the location box, type "telnet://" (but do not type the quote marks) and the Internet address (example:telnet://freenet.columbus.oh.us). This will automatically launch the telnet program for you (see Figure B.5).

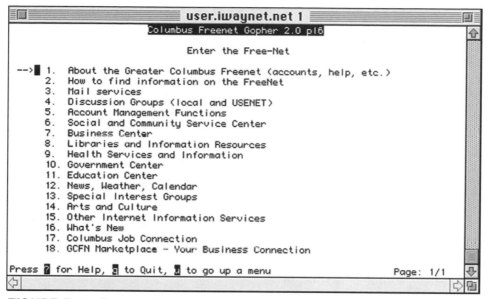

**FIGURE B.5   Greater Columbus Freenet accessed through telnet**

When initiating telnet sessions, you may need to know a login and password. Most lists or books containing telnet addresses give this information. In some cases the host site will tell you the login and the password.

```
131.187.116.238

            WELCOME TO THE DISCOVERY PLACE
                 ON-LINE CATALOG
               ( 2175 - $TSEO.#W151 )

   To search enter one of the following commands:

   A/Author-name   to find items by author name
   T/Title         to find items by title
   S/Subject       to find items by subject
   KW              to find items by WORD or NAME or to COMBINE words

   AV              to see your reserves/checkouts/fines

   Or use one of the following special commands:

        HOME   to start again at this screen
        MENU   to return to the menu of available
               services
        HELP   to see a list of all commands and how
               to make your searches more specific
        Note:  If your terminal is idle for 8 minutes,
>>
```

**FIGURE B.6   Online Library Catalog accessed through telnet**

*Example:*

login: guest

password: guest

The host may also ask for the type of terminal emulation you are using. The most commonly used type of terminal emulation is VT100.

*Example:*

TERM = (unknown) > VT100

## Telnet Step-by-Step Instructions

Step 1.    In the location box of your Web browser, type: telnet://internet address (example: telnet://freenet.columbus.oh.us)

Step 2.    login: type the login

Step 3.    password: type in the password

Step 4.    TERM= (unknown) > VT100 [terminal emulation]

If your screen freezes or you are unable to exit a telnet host, you can escape with these commands:

To escape telnet

1. type ^] (control-right bracket)

2. telnet> **q**

# FTP

FTP (file transfer protocol) allows you to transfer files from one computer to another. Files are stored at the remote site in directories. To gain access and download files, you must initiate an anonymous FTP session and change directories, or type the directory path until you reach the file you want to transfer (see Figures B.7 and B.8).

There are two types of files that can be transferred: ASCII (text) and binary (graphics, formatted documents, and software programs). Another way you may access FTP sites is through your Web browser. When you use this method, you simply click on the file and it automatically downloads to your hard drive.

# FTP Step-by-Step Instructions for Downloading

Step 1.    In your FTP program, type in the server or host name.

Step 2.    Type in the directory path if you know it.

Step 3.    Username: type the word "anonymous".

Step 4.    Password: type in your e-mail address.

Step 5.    Locate the file to download and double click on it.

You may also want to upload files after you create home pages. Your Internet Service Provider may provide you with space for these pages and provide you with a login and password.

```
┌─────────────────────────────────────────────┐
│ ═══════════ New Connection... ═══════════    │
│                                               │
│  Enter host name, userid, and password (or   │
│  choose from the shortcut menu):              │
│                                               │
│  Host:        ┌──────────────────────────┐   │
│               │ ftp.iwaynet.net          │   │
│               └──────────────────────────┘   │
│  User ID:     ┌──────────────────────────┐   │
│               │ your_username            │   │
│               └──────────────────────────┘   │
│  Password:    ┌──────────────────────────┐   │
│               │ •••••••••                │   │
│               └──────────────────────────┘   │
│  Directory:   ┌──────────────────────────┐   │
│               │ |                        │   │
│               └──────────────────────────┘   │
│  Shortcuts:   ▼     ( Cancel )    ( OK )      │
└─────────────────────────────────────────────┘
```

*FIGURE B.7  Making a Connection Using Fetch for Macintosh*

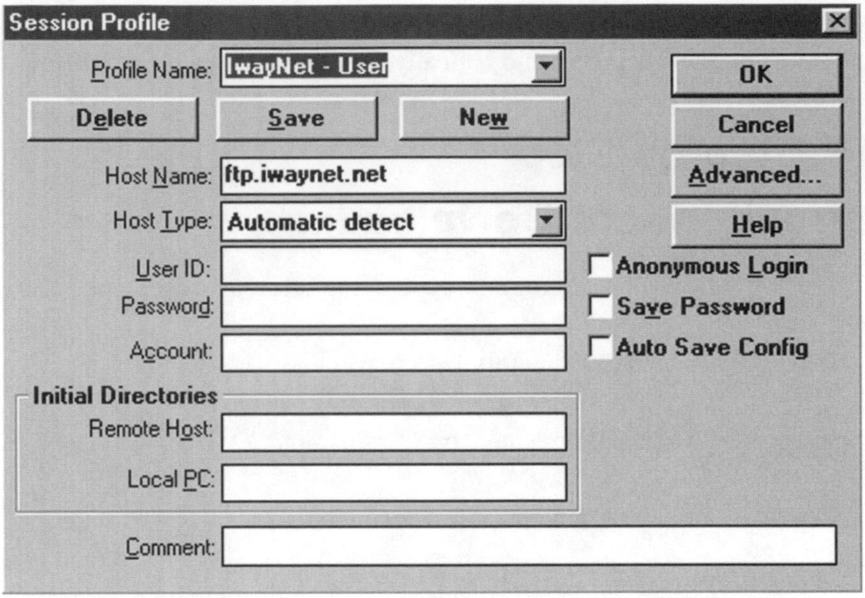

**FIGURE B.8   Making a Connection Using WS_FTP for Windows**

# FTP Step-by-Step
# Instructions for Uploading

Step 1.   In your FTP program, type the server or host name.

Step 2.   Type in the directory path.

Step 3.   Username: type in your login name.

Step 4.   Password: type in your password.

Step 5.   Select the files you want to upload and use the put command or the right arrow (see Figure B.9 and B.10).

Files with the html or htm extension should be transferred as ASCII text and files with the .gif or .jpg extension should be transferred as binary or raw data.

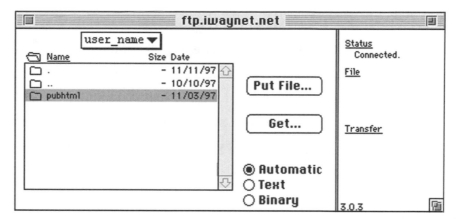

*FIGURE B.9   File Transfer Using Fetch for Macintosh*

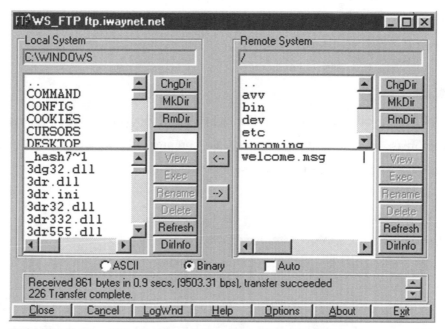

*FIGURE B.10   File Transfer Using WS_FTP for Windows*

# Compression Utility Programs

Each file that you download has an extension. Many of these are compressed to save storage space and limit the download time. For example, .tar, .zip, and .sit can contain several small files within a larger file. You need a program to decompress the files after you download them to your hard drive. Once a compression program is set up and configured to work with your Web browser, the files will be automatically decompressed.

## Windows

Most files for Windows are compressed as zip files. PKZip (http://www.pkware.com) and Winzip (http://www.winzip.com) are utility programs for decompressing these files.

## Macintosh

The commercial software program Stuffit Deluxe is one of the best packages for coding, decoding, stuffing, and unstuffing Macintosh files. Stuffit Expander and DropStuff are smaller freeware and shareware versions available on the Internet (http://www.aladdinsys.com).

## UNIX

UNIX files have the extension .Z attached to the filename. These files can be decompressed at your host site. You can also compress files to save storage space.

At the system prompt> type uncompress filename.Z

*Example:*

uncompress history.Z

To compress a file to save storage space:

At the system prompt> type compress filename

*Example:*

compress history

After compressing the file, it will have the .Z extension again.

## Guide for File Transfer

| File Extension | Transfer Type | Computer | Program |
|---|---|---|---|
| .bin | binary | Macintosh | executable |
| .cpt | binary | Macintosh | compact pro |
| .hqx | ASCII | Macintosh | BinHex ur Stuffit Expander |
| .sea | binary | Macintosh | self-extracting |
| .sit | binary | Macintosh | Stuffit Expander |
| .gz | binary | UNIX | gunzip |
| .tar | binary | UNIX | tar command |
| .uue | ASCII | UNIX | uudecude command |
| .Z | binary | UNIX | uncompress |
| .arc | binary | PC | pkarc |
| .com | binary | PC | executable |
| .exe | binary | PC | executable |
| .zip | binary | PC | pkzip or winzip |
| .gif | binary (graphics) | All | gif viewing programs |
| .jpg | binary (graphics) | All | jpeg viewing programs |
| .pdf | binary | All | Adobe Acrobat |
| .ps | ASCII | All | postscript printer |
| .txt | ASCII | All | text editor |

# NEWS STREAMING

With Educast, a free screensaver for Windows and Macintosh (see figure B.11), updates from the Internet are automatically downloaded for you. You decide what information you want and then view it off-line at your convenience. Ready-to-use activity sheets, grant ideas, timely articles, and high-quality education sites are a few examples of the information available through Educast (http://www. educast.com).

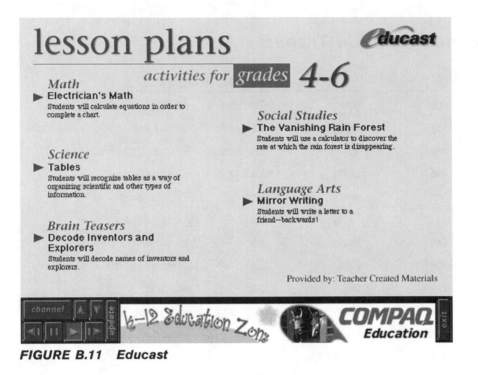

**FIGURE B.11   Educast**

Once you have installed the program and are connected to the Internet, follow these steps:

1. Move your cursor to the "sleepcorner" of your screen (upper right for Windows, left for Macintosh) to start the Educast screen saver.

2. Click the Update button in the lower left. Educast will automatically access your browser and download the latest available news and resources.

3. Use the navigation buttons at the lower left to surf through the channels.

4. Use the Exit button at the lower left to turn Educast off.

5. Customize the settings by using the Educast Control Panel available from the Educast icon in Windows and the Apple Menu for Macintosh.

# TELECONFERENCING

Sharing ideas and files in real time is made possible through a variety of hardware and software. With Timbuktu Pro for Macintosh and NetMeeting for Windows, you can share files, look at computer screens, and have online discussions between remote sites. Using a miniature camera such as the Connectix QuickCam and CUSeeMe, you can videoconference with another person over the Internet.

• Timbuktu Pro (http://www.netopia.com/software/tb2/mac)

• NetMeeting (http://www.microsoft.com/netmeeting)

• Connectix (http://www.connectix.com)

• Enhanced CUSeeMe—White Pine (http://www.wpine.com/products/ cu-seeme)

Once you are logged on to the Internet, follow these instructions for making a CUSeeMe connection.

Step 1.    Select Connect from the Conference Menu (see Figure B.12.).

**FIGURE B.12**

Step 2.    Type in an IP address (see Figure B.13.). An IP address is the
address for the computer you wish to connect with on the
Internet. If you do not have an individual IP address, you can
connect to a reflector IP that allows multiple connections at the
same time (see Figure B.13.).

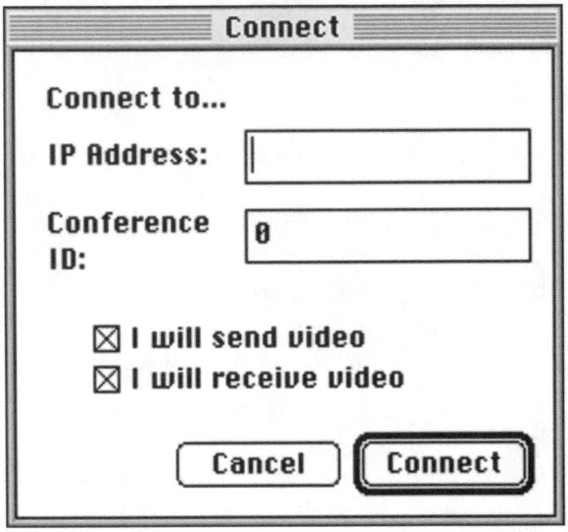

**Connect**

Connect to...

IP Address:

Conference ID:    θ

☒ I will send video
☒ I will receive video

Cancel    Connect

*FIGURE B.13*

Step 3.    Each person connected will see a window appear with his or
her name at the top (see Figure B.14.).

LINDA

3.2 fps        18 Kbps

*FIGURE B.14*

Step 4.    To talk, hold down on the Push to Talk button (see Figure B.15.).

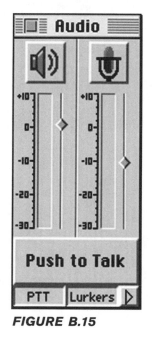

**FIGURE B.15**

Step 5.    Choose File and Quit to end the CUSeeMe program (see Figure B.16.).

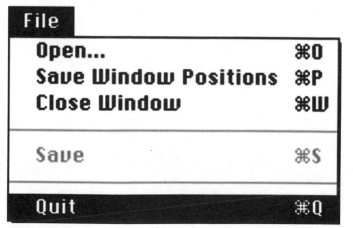

**FIGURE B.16**

# Electronic Publishing

You can initiate projects and share ideas on the Internet by becoming an information provider.

## TIPS FOR GETTING STARTED

- Find a place to post your information such as your school server or an Internet provider that is directly connected to the Internet.

- Decide how elaborate a design you want. It is easy to post text on the Net. More time and effort are involved with images, sound, and video.

- If you want to create files for the World Wide Web, you will need to know how to write in HTML (Hypertext Markup Language). It is not difficult to learn and will give your information added flair when you include color icons, images, sound, and video.

- Carefully plan what information you want to share with others and how it will be arranged for easy access and understanding.

- Consider using an HTML editor or converter to prepare information for the World Wide Web.

## Some Good Sources for Web Publishing

- http://dir.yahoo.com/Computers_and_Internet/Internet/World_Wide_Web/
- http://online.anu.edu.au/CNIP/authors/
- http://www.webcom.com/~webcom/html/

*Teach Yourself Web Publishing with HTML in a Week* by Laura Lemay and published by SAMS Publishing is a very comprehensive source with lots of examples and exercises to follow.

# GUIDE FOR MAKING A SCHOOL HOME PAGE

Where do you begin when you want to create a home page for your school? You've probably heard it is easy with one of the drag-and-drop HTML editing programs such as Adobe Pagemill or Claris Home Page. You may have been told you can construct one in about five minutes.

It is a little more involved than what you have heard or been told. There are a few things you need to know first before you jump into making a home page. As with any good project, organization and understanding of the end product is very important.

## Design Elements

Think of a home page as if it were a book or magazine. In a publication you are targeting a specific audience. You want your work to be eye catching, easy to navigate, and interesting enough so that your readers will return. Let's take a look at some examples:

- Fairland Elementary School - Montgomery County, Maryland
  (http://www.wam.umd.edu/~toh/Fairland.html)

- Greentown Elementary School—North Canton, Ohio
  (http://viking.stark.k12.oh.us/~greentown/)

- Hopkinton Middle and High Schools—Contoocook, New Hampshire
  (http://www.conknet.com/hhs/)

- Poudre High School—Ft. Collins, Colorado
  (http://www.psd.k12.co.us/schools/phs/)

- Wai'anae High School—The Island of Oahu Hawaii
  (http://www.aloha.net/~waianhi/)

# Content

Spend some time deciding what main links you want to create on your front page. You might want to include a mission statement, parent area, staff directory, activities, or calendar. Storyboard your Web site so you will understand how everything fits together.

Answer these questions:

1. Who are your customers?

2. What information do you want to provide to them? Make a list.

3. Do you need to have an area for parents?

4. How will the information be organized?

# Before You Begin

Before you begin you should collect photographs for scanning and type your content information in a word processing program.

1. Keep all of your files in one folder. This will make it easier to link files and eliminate errors when you load the page to the server. The biggest mistake beginners make is in the linking process.

2. Name files in lowercase for simplicity. This will help eliminate problems when loading files to a UNIX server. UNIX is case sensitive.

3. Keep file names short and meaningful. The rule of thumb is eight characters plus the file extension. There should be no spaces.

4. Save Text Files: filename.html (Macintosh); filename.htm (DOS &Windows).

5. Save Image Files: filename.gif. Be sure you have a graphics program that allows you to save your images in the correct format.

6. Save your front page as index.html.

# Ten Tips for Webmasters

1. Keep it simple, small, and short. Keep the size of your pages small. No one wants to wait five minutes for a page to load. Try to keep the load time within thirty seconds for your home page.

2. Provide enough information on your home page so the reader will know about your site and what is available there. (consider storyboarding your information before constructing your pages.)

3. Use Courier or Monaco 10-point type for the body of the text. Save the file as text-only in a word processor with the extension .html or .htm on DOS. You can also use an HTML editor.

4. Gif images should be no bigger than 20K; 2″ x 2″ for a square or 1.5″ x 3″ for a rectangle are good examples. Create thumbnail images that link to larger images on separate pages. Show the amount of K for each of the larger pictures so the reader will know the approximate load time.

5. Keep in mind the width of the page when designing the size of logos. Readers will have various computer screen sizes. If the logo is too wide they will have to scroll in order to see all of it.

6. Provide new information on a regular basis so readers will return. You might want to design interactive projects, links to changing information, or curriculum materials such as lesson plans.

7. Avoid long lists of links to other sites.

8. Each additional page should point back to the home page.

9. Provide an e-mail address or contact information for comments from readers.

10. Avoid publishing personal information.

# Design Tools

These links will assist both the beginner and advanced Webmaster.

## Animated Gif Software

- GifBuilder—Macintosh
  (http://iawww.epfl.ch/staff/yves.piguet/clip2gifhome/gifbuilder.html)

- Gif Construction Set—Windows
  (http://www.mindworkshop.com/alchemy/gifcon.html)

## Background Color and Designs

- ColorMaker
  (http://www.bagism.com/colormaker/)

- Windy's Design Studio
  (http://www.windyweb.com/design/index.html)

## Graphic Conversion

- Lview Pro—Windows
  (http://www.lview.com/)

- GraphicConverter—Macintosh
  (http://www.goldinc.com/Lemke/gc.html)

## Guestbook

- Matt's Script Archive
  (http://www.worldwidemart.com/scripts/)

- SPiN Goodies: Multi Guest Book
  (http://www.spin.de/)

## HTML Quick Reference Guides

- Bare Bones Guide to HTML
  (http://werbach.com/barebones/)

- Sevloid Guide to HTML
  (http://www.powerup.com.au/~sevloid/webtips/sevhtml.htm)

## Images or Icons

- Graphic Station
  (http://www.geocities.com/SiliconValley/6603/)

- Billy Bear's ClipArt
  (http://www.billybear4kids.com/)

## JavaScript

- JavaScript World
  (http://www.jsworld.com/)

- Cut and Paste JavaScript
  (http://www.infohiway.com/javascript/indexf.htm)

## Music—Midi Files

- Classical Music Files
  (http://www.prs.net/midi.html)

- Disney Music Page
  (http://www.dismusic.com)

- Halloween Midi Page
  (http://www.bestweb.net/~wallnut/halloween/midis.html)

## Web Pages in Minutes

- Filamentality
  (http://www.kn.pacbell.com/wired/fil/)

- WebSpawner
  (http://www.webspawner.com/)

- Web Wizard—Windows
  (http://www.halcyon.com/artamedia/webwizard/)

# HTML

Hypertext Markup Language formats items in a document so a Web browser can read them. This allows you to publish on the Web. HTML uses tags to do this formatting. The tags work in pairs—one to begin < >, the other to end < /> . Tags can be typed in upper- or lowercase letters. You can use a word processing program or an HTML editor to construct a home page.

## Beginning and Ending Tags

The following examples will show how a page is created and then how it will look in a browser. Each page begins with these four tags: <HTML>, <HEAD><TITLE></TITLE></HEAD>, and <BODY>.

### *<HTML>*

This tag tells the browser it is a hypertext markup language document.

### *<HEAD><TITLE></TITLE></HEAD>*

Within the Head tag is the Title tag. You insert the words you want to appear in the title bar of the browser. Suppose you want your school name to appear in the title bar, you would type in your school name.

*Example:*

<HEAD><TITLE>School Name</TITLE></HEAD>

Figure C.1 shows how your school name would appear in the browser.

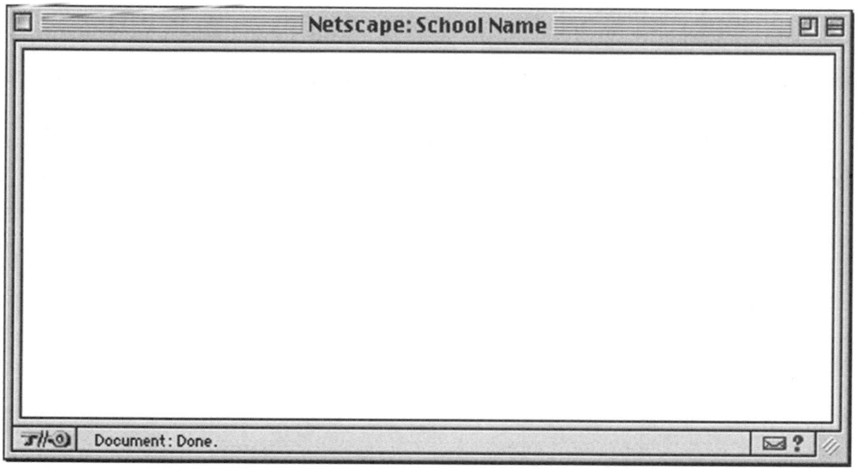

*FIGURE C.1*

### *<BODY>*

The content of your page is placed between the body tags. Content includes text, pictures, sounds, videoclips, and other items you want viewers to experience. Each page ends with the closing body tag and the closing HTML tag:

</BODY>
</HTML>

## Image Tag

The first item you might like to have on your page is a picture of your school or mascot. The type of images used on the Web are called GIF (pronounced like the peanut butter brand name) or JPEG. If you take a picture with a 35mm point-and-shoot camera, you will need to have the film processed and then digitize the picture. This simply means converting the paper picture into a format that the computer can read. This can be done by scanning the photo. Or you can request that your photographs be digitized on a CD-ROM. Ask your local film processing retailer how that can be done.

Seattle Filmworks (http://www.filmworks.com) is a mail order vendor that will process and convert all of your photographs to a computer disk. They process all 35mm films, including Kodak, Konica, Fuji, and Agfa. For about $16.00, you will receive negatives, prints, a computer disk (Macintosh or Windows) your photographs, and an index sheet (small proofs of all your pictures) along with viewing software. If you decide to purchase their film, you will *only* be able to have it processed by Seattle Filmworks because they use a different chemical process than local film processing stores.

Another way to include a photograph of your school is by taking a picture with a digital camera. Then, import the image directly into a computer graphics program.

Whatever method you use, remember to save the photograph as a GIF or JPEG image file.

Now add an image to your document.

## *<IMG SRC="filename.gif">*

The image tag allows you to add a picture to your home page. You would replace filename.gif with the name of your GIF image (example: <IMG SRC ="school.gif">). Figure C.2 shows how it would look.

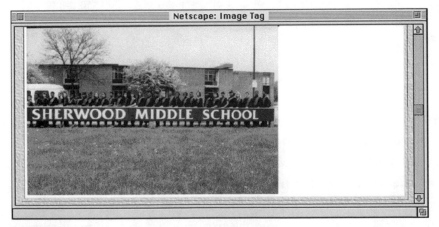

**FIGURE C.2**

Notice the picture appears on the left side of the screen. You would probably like to have it centered. You can place the picture in the center of the page by putting the <Center> tag around the image tag (<CENTER><IMG SRC= "school.gif"> </CETER>). Now the picture appears in the center of the page (see Figure C.3).

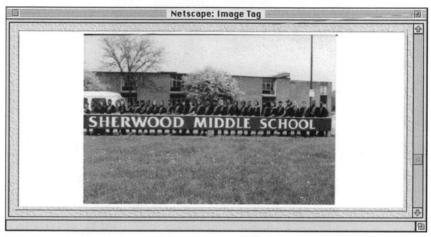

**FIGURE C.3**

# Headers and Line Breaks

Under the picture, you will want the school name, address, and telephone number. Before you type the text, think about the spacing between the picture and the text. To put a line of space, you can use the paragraph <P> tag. Place a paragraph tag after the image tag.

<IMG SRC="school.gif">

<P>

Next you need to determine what size of text to use for the header. There are six sizes of header tags with <H1> being the largest and <H6> being the smallest. You will want your school name to be large, so use <H1> . You can always change it to a smaller header tag later if you don't like the way it looks on the page. To separate one line from another insert a line break <BR> tag. It is different from the paragraph tag because there is no space between the lines.

<CENTER><H1>School Name

<BR> School Address

<BR> City, State, Zip Code

<BR> Telephone Number </H1></CENTER>

*FIGURE C.4*

To separate the picture and school information from the rest of the content on the front page, use the horizontal rule tag, <HR>. This will place a shaded line across the page.

<CENTER><H1>School Name

<BR> School Address

<BR> City, State, Zip Code

<BR> Telephone Number </H1></CENTER> <P>

<HR>

Your page will look like Figure C.4 after inserting and centering the school information.

# Adding Links to Your School Page

Links take you to another page. There are internal links, sometimes called local files, and external links. Internal links are files you create and keep on your own server. External links are links to other Web sites on the Internet.

The link tag is <A HREF="""></A> The local filename or http address is inserted between the quotation marks. The linked text that appears on the screen is placed between the right and left arrows ><.

## Internal Link

Let's say you create another page about your mission statement and name the file mission.html (see Figure C.5). On the front page you would create a link to go to that page by typing:

<A HREF="mission.html">Mission Statement</A>

*FIGURE C.5*

## External Link

Most of the links on your front page will probably go to local files. However, to illustrate how to create an external link, assume you want your home page visitors to go to another Web site such as the Eisenhower National Clearinghouse (see Figure C.6 on page 166). You would type the following:

<A HREF="http://www.enc.org">Eisenhower National Clearinghouse</A>

## Increasing the Text Size

The text will appear with an underline indicating it is a link to another page (see Figure C.7 on page 166). Since the standard HTML text is small, add the <H3></H3> tag around the text to make it larger. <H3><A HREF="http://www.enc.org"> Eisenhower National Clearinghouse</A></H3>

**FIGURE C.6**

**FIGURE C.7**

## Indenting Text

To indent the text, use the unordered list tag (see Figure C.8).

    &lt;UL&gt; &lt;H3&gt;&lt;A HREF="mission.html"&gt;Mission Statement&lt;/A&gt;&lt;/H3&gt;
    &lt;BR&gt;
    &lt;H3&gt;&lt;A HREF="http://www.enc.org"&gt;Eisenhower National
      Clearinghouse&lt;/A&gt;&lt;/H3&gt;
    &lt;/UL&gt;

*FIGURE C.8*

## E-Mail Link

You should add a contact address so visitors to your site can make comments. Create a link to your e-mail address. You will need to know your own e-mail address. The following is simply an example.

    &lt;A HREF="MAILTO:username@columbus.k12.oh.us"&gt;
        username@columbus.k12.oh.us&lt;/A&gt;

# Adding Background Colors

The front page to this point looks plain. To jazz up the appearance, experiment with different colors or backgrounds. There is an array of colors to use and several Web-based programs can assist you with choosing colors. One such program that is popular is ColorMaker.

You can choose colors for background (the color of the page), text (the color of the text on your page), link (the color of the underlined text for a link before you click on it), visited link (the color of the underlined text after you have been to the linked site), and active link (the color that blinks when you click on an underlined text link).

To add these colors, you place them inside the body tag; the colors are expressed in hexadecimal code.

<BODY BGCOLOR="#CC9933" TEXT="#000000" LINK="#CC3300"
VLINK="#663300" ALINK="#0066CC">

Your page would look like the example in Figure C.9.

*FIGURE C.9*

# Tables

The <Table></Table> tag is a good way to create columns on a home page. Each Table has rows <TR></TR> and columns <TD></TD>. Suppose you want to have two columns of links, here is how you would create the table.

```
<TABLE>
<TR><TD>About Us</TD><TD>Staff Directory</TD></TR>
<TR><TD>Events Calendar</TD><TD>Departments or
Programs</TD></TR>
<TR><TD>Student Projects</TD><TD>Community Partnerships or
        Parent Information</TD></TR>
</TABLE>
```

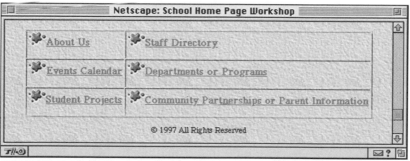

**FIGURE C.10 Both columns and rows line up neatly on the page**

# HOME PAGE TEMPLATE

You can use this template to create your school page by retyping it or by downloading it from: (http://www.cyberbee.com/schoolpage/school.html). The directions are embedded right in the template so you will know when and where to insert your own information. Simply use any word processing program to make changes and then save the changes as a text file with the htm or html extension. You can use Simple Text for Macintosh or Word Pad for Windows. Once you have a better understanding of HTML, you may want to use an editing program.

Here's a rundown of how to format the home page:

```
<HTML>
<!— Put your school name between the title tags —>
<HEAD><TITLE>School Home Page Workshop</TITLE></HEAD>
<!— The body tag allows you to add a color or image background. It also
        allows you to set colors for the text of your document and link colors.
        Use Color Maker, an interactive Web site to select the colors for your
        page. After you make your color selections, it returns the code that is
        to be placed in the body tag.—>
```

<BODY BACKGROUND="jpbac.gif" TEXT="#000033" LINK="#FF0 000" VLINK="#0000FF" ALINK="#FF0000" >

<!— Replace blue2.gif with your school picture in this tag. Remember to have good lighting and have some students and teachers in the picture so that it will be attractive to those visiting your page. After you have taken your photograph, you can scan it and save it as a GIF image in a graphics program. If you use a digital camera, simply import it into your program and save it as a GIF. —>

<CENTER><!— Graphic Tag —><IMG SRC="blue2.gif"></CENTER>

<P>

<!— Put in your school name, street address, city, state, zip, and telephone number. —>

<CENTER><H2>School Name

<BR>Street Address

<BR>City, State Zip Code

<BR>Telephone Number</H2></CENTER>

<P>

<HR>

<P>

<!— This is your main list of links. Most of these will be internal links to other pages. Although I have created the link tag, it goes nowhere. You will have to create those pages depending on the content you want to include. Feel free to add more items or change those listed. This is a template to help you get started. You can also replace the images with those of your own choosing. Graphic Station is a great place to find images. Web Explosion, a commercial product for both Macintosh and Windows, is available from many of the computer software mail order catalogs. I purchased mine from Mac Warehouse. —>

<UL>

<H3><!— Graphic Tag —><IMG SRC="red.gif"><!— Link Tag —><A HREF="about.html">About Us</A></H3>

<P>

```
<H3><!— Graphic Tag —><IMG SRC="red.gif"><!— Link Tag —><A
HREF="about.html">Staff Directory</A></H3>
<P>
<H3><!— Graphic Tag —><IMG SRC="red.gif"><!— Link Tag —><A
HREF="about.html">Events Calendar</A></H3>
<P>
<H3><!— Graphic Tag —><IMG SRC="red.gif"><!— Link Tag —><A
HREF="about.html">Departments or Programs</A></H3>
<P>
<H3><!— Graphic Tag —><IMG SRC="red.gif"><!— Link Tag —><A
HREF="about.html">Student Projects</A></H3>
<P>
<H3><!— Graphic Tag —><IMG SRC="red.gif"><!— Link Tag —><A
HREF="about.html">Community Partnerships or Parent Information</A>
        </H3>
</UL>
<!— This is the same information only in the table format. —>
<P>
<CENTER><TABLE border=1>
<TR><TD><H3><!— Graphic Tag —><IMG SRC="red.gif"><!—Link
        Tag —><A
HREF="about.html">About Us</A></H3></TD>
<TD><H3><!— Graphic Tag —><IMG SRC="red.gif"><!— Link Tag —
><A
HREF="about.html">Staff Directory</A></H3></TD></TR>
<TR>
<TD><H3><!— Graphic Tag —><IMG SRC="red.gif"><!— Link Tag
        —><A HREF="about.html">Events Calendar</A></H3></TD>
<TD><H3><!— Graphic Tag —><IMG SRC="red.gif"><!—Link  Tag—
        ><A
HREF="about.html">Departments or Programs</A></H3></TD></TR>
<TR>
```

```
<TD><H3><!—Graphic Tag —><IMG SRC="red.gif"><!—Link Tag—
    ><A
HREF="about.html">Student Projects</A></H3></TD>
<TD><H3><!—Graphic Tag —><IMG SRC="red.gif"><!—Link Tag—
    ><A
HREF="about.html">Community Partnerships or Parent Information
    </A></H3></TD></TR>
</TABLE></CENTER>
<P>
<CENTER>&copy; 1997 All Rights Reserved</CENTER>
<P>
<!— You can replace the image tag with one you choose. Or you can
    use the horizontal rule tag <HR> —>
<CENTER><!—Graphic Tag—><IMG SRC="animline.gif"></CENTER>
<P>
<!— It's really nice to know when someone updates the page. —>
<CENTER>Updated March 15, 1997</CENTER>
<!— Replace the information after MAILTO: with your own e-mail address.
    Replace the words "your e-mail address" with your actual address, your
    name, or the school's name depending on whose address you use. —>
<P>
<CENTER>For comments or more information contact:
<!— MailTo  Tag  —><A  HREF="MAILTO:jdoe@osu.edu">your  e-mail
    address</A></CENTER>
<!— Remember to save your main file as index.html. That's all you need to
    start out. As you become more experienced, you will want to add other
    features to your page. You may even want to use an HTML editing pro-
    gram. —>
</BODY>
</HTML>
```

# HTML Tags

## General Tags

| | | |
|---|---|---|
| <html> | </html> | complete HTML document |
| <head> | </head> | main header |
| <title> | </title> | title of the document |
| <body> | </body> | most of the document is included in the body |

## Headers

| | | |
|---|---|---|
| <h1> | </h1> | first level heading and most prominent |
| <h2> | </h2> | second level heading |
| <h3> | </h3> | third level heading |
| <h4> | </h4> | fourth level heading |
| <h5> | </h5> | fifth level heading |
| <h6> | </h6> | sixth level heading |

## Text

| | | |
|---|---|---|
| <p> | | paragraph with space below the text |
| <br> | | line break with no extra space below the text |
| <hr> | | horizontal rule |
| <pre> | </pre> | preformatted text |
| <em> | </em> | emphasized text |
| <blockquote> | </blockquote> | quotation |
| <dfn> | </dfn> | definition |
| <cite> | </cite> | citation |
| <b> | </b> | bold |
| <i> | </i> | italics |
| <u> | </u> | underline |
| <tt> | </tt> | typewriter font |

## *Image*

<img src="image.gif">                    designate a picture

## *Anchors*

&lt;a href="URL"&gt;link name&lt;/a&gt;            link to another file
&lt;a name="target"&gt;&lt;/a&gt;                 location in a document
&lt;a href="#anchor name"&gt;link name&lt;/a&gt;   link to a location in the same file
&lt;a href="URL#target"&gt;&lt;/a&gt;              link to a location in another file

## *Lists*

### Ordered List—
### Labeled with a Number Sequentially

&lt;ol&gt;                      Begins a numbered list
&lt;li&gt;                      First item will be labeled with a number 1
&lt;li&gt;                      Next item will be labeled with a number 2
&lt;/ol&gt;                     Ends a numbered list

### Unordered List—Preceded by a Bullet or Marker

&lt;ul&gt;                      Begins a list that can be in any order
&lt;li&gt;                      First item is preceded by a bullet or marker
&lt;li&gt;                      Second item is preceded by a bullet or marker
&lt;/ul&gt;                     Ends the unordered list

### Glossary List

&lt;dl&gt;                      Begins the listing
&lt;dt&gt;                      First term
&lt;dd&gt;                      Term defined
&lt;dt&gt;                      Second term
&lt;dd&gt;                      Second term defined
&lt;/dl&gt;                     Ends the listing

# Glossary

**Analog**. Signals used in voice or music. These are continuous signals sent over telephone lines.

**Archie.** A client program that allows the user to search FTP sites.

**Baud rate.** The rate at which data is transmitted over a telephone line. 28.8, 33.6 and 56 kbps (kilobits per second) are commonly used.

**Bit.** The most basic unit of data that can be recognized by a computer, either a "0" or a "1."

**Browser.** Software program such as Netscape or Internet Explorer used to access the World Wide Web.

**Client software.** Programs running on your computer that transfer information to and from a server. Eudora (e-mail) and Fetch (FTP) are examples of client software.

**Demodulate.** Conversion of an analog signal to a digital signal.

**Digital, binary.** A signal that is comprised of a 1 or 0, either on or off. It is not continuous.

**DNS.** Domain Name Server.

**Download.** Transferring a file from the host computer to your computer.

**E-mail.** Electronic messages sent from one person to another via computer networks such as the Internet.

**FAQ.** Frequently asked questions.

**Flame.** Critical remark made by someone about something posted on a news or discussion group.

**FTP.** File Transfer Protocol is a function that allows the user (client) to get files from a remote computer (host).

**Gopher.** A menu-driven program that will automatically make FTP and telnet connections to global networks. Many Freenets use the Gopher system.

**Host computer.** The computer that provides information over a network.

**HTML.** Hypertext Markup Language, the code used to create a document on the World Wide Web.

**Http.** Hypertext transfer protocol, the standard prefix used for addresses on the World Wide Web.

**Internet address.** The series of numbers or letters that identifies the site of the host computer. The suffix of the address often helps users know what kind of service they are connected to on the network. Internet addresses are used for FTP, telnet, gopher, and e-mail. Example: Heartland Free-Net: heartland.bradley.edu (136.176.5.114).

**ISDN.** Integrated Services Digital Network offers a higher speed—between 64 and 128 kbps—on a dial-up connection between 64 kbps and 128 kbps.

**IP.** Internet Protocol, the standard way in which all computers communicate over the Internet.

**ISP.** Internet Service Provider, a company that allows a direct connection to the Internet using PPP (Point to Point Protocol). Examples include national companies like AT&T WorldNet and Mindspring. There are also many local companies that provide the same services. Generally you pay a flat-rate monthly fee for full Internet access twenty-four hours a day.

**Listserv.** A brand of software used for online discussion groups that is often used generically to describe online groups focused on a particular area of interest; subscribed to via e-mail.

**Lurker.** Someone who subscribes to a discussion group but does not participate. Some groups sponsor unlurking days.

**MIME.** Multipurpose Internet Mail Extension. An extension to an e-mail program that allows the transfer of nontext data such as graphics.

**Modem.** A piece of hardware that acts as a translator between computers and telephone lines.

**Modulate.** Conversion of a digital signal to an analog signal.

**MUD.** Multi-user domain; online virtual reality.

**MOO.** Object oriented MUD.

**Newbie.** Someone new to the Internet.

**OPAC.** Online Public Access Catalog. Library catalogs that have been computerized.

**PPP.** Point-to-Point Protocol, a connection over a dial-up phone line to a service provider that allows direct connection to the Internet.

**RFC.** Request for Comments document.

**Server.** The host computer on a network that stores information.

**SMTP.** Simple Mail Transfer Protocol. The Internet standard for transferring electronic messages from one computer to another.

**Spam or spamming.** Stuffing someone's mailbox with the same message numerous times, which causes the mail system to crash; or posting a lengthy message to the whole group that should be sent directly to an individual. Unsolicited e-mail. Mailbombs.

**T1.** A high speed line at 1.544 mbs.

**T3.** A high speed line at 44.736 mbs.

**TCP/IP.** Transmission Control Protocol/Internet Protocol allows data to be transferred between two networks using the same protocol or language. Software settings on your workstation must be configured to work with either your school network or an Internet Service Provider.

**Telnet.** A program that connects the user to a host computer with an interactive welcome screen. Telnet sessions allow the user to view information on a host computer as though the user were sitting at its terminal.

**Terminal emulation.** Allows the client (user) computer to communicate with the host computer in the same language.

**Under construction.** A term used for Web pages that are being built or revised.

**Upload.** Transferring a file from the client (user) computer to the host computer.

**URL.** Uniform Resource Locator. An expression of an Internet address, including the protocol. Example for the World Wide Web: http://www.cyberbee.com. Example for telnet: telnet://freenet.columbus.oh.us. Example for FTP: ftp://ftp.route-66.net

**Veronica.** Allows the user to search and find topics in gopherspace.

**WHOIS.** A searchable directory of people and their Internet addresses.

**Webmaster.** The person who maintains a World Wide Web server.

# Subjects

## A

Abilock, Debbie, 18
acceptable use policies, 97–104
access, Internet, 109–115
activities, 30–31
    art, 27–28, 66–67, 73
    butterfly, 81
    classroom exchange, 32
    economic, 29
    flight, 76-77
    foreign countries, 82–83
    fun, 66–68
    gardening, 81–82
    general, 61–63
    geography, 49–50
    health and nutrition, 31
    language arts, 32–35, 68–74
    math, 35–38, 63–64, 74–75
    music, 38–39
    news, 83–85
    online greeting cards, 65
    publishing, 74
    rain forest, 80–81
    reference, 85–87
    science, 39–45, 76–82
    social studies, 45–59, 82–85
    weather, 78–80
    Web postcards, 64–65
    writing, 72–73
addresses
    e-mail, 133
    extensions, 133–134
Adobe Acrobat Reader, 119
ADSL (Asymmetric Digital Subscriber Service), 114
aerodynamics. *See* flight
African Americans, 45–47, 49, 57
airplanes, paper, 76–77. *See also* flight
algebra, 37. *See also* math
America Online, 111, 115

American frontier, 55–58, 64
American Indians. *See* Native Americans
American Master Teacher Program, 39
animals, 41, 44, 66. *See also* birds; wildlife
animation, 73
Anthony, Susan B., 59
AOL (America Online), 111, 115
APA (American Psychological Association) style
    guide for citing electronic resources, 17
architecture, 28
art, 27–28, 66–67, 73
    African, 46
    clip, 29
    first ladies' portraits, 51
    presidential portraits, 51
Asia, lesson plans on, 54
Askew, Jim, 13
assignment organizer, 13–15
astronomy, 40, 43, 45, 62, 77–78
Asymmetric Digital Subscriber Service (ADSL), 114
attachments, e-mail, 137
audio plug-ins, 119–120
authors, 32–35, 69–71
Avi, 69
awards
    Caldecott, 33
    Newbery, 34

## B

Beaty, Bill, 40
bees, 40. *See also* insects
Berkowitz, Robert E., 1, 3
Betsy Ross, 86
Bialo, E. R., 90
bibliographic guides, 17–19

Big6 Skills, 1–15
biographies, 47
biology, 40, 42, 63
birds, wild, 68. *See also* animals; wildlife
bison, 55
blocking software, 107–108
Blume, Judy, 69
books, 32–35, 71–72
    authors, 69–71
    making, 71, 72
    pop-up, 71, 72
Boolean searches, 6
botanical gardens, 42
Brady, Matthew, 49
Breen, Patrick, 58
Brett, Jan, 65, 69
browser software, 91–95, 116, 117
buffalo, 55
Burkett, Jalyn, 56
butterflies, 81. *See also* insects
Byars, Betsy, 69
Byzantine studies, 53


# C

cable modems, 114
calculators, 36, 37, 38
Caldecott Award, 33
capturing Web pages, 91–95
cards, online greeting, 65
cartooning, 73. *See also* art
Catt, Carrie Chapman, 59
cave art, French, 28
celebrities, 47
Chang, Christopher, 89
Chauvet cave art, 28
chemistry, 40
children's literature, 32–35
citation, Internet, 12, 16–19
citing electronic resources, 12, 16–19
Civil War, 48–49
classical music composers, 38
Clayton, William Clayton, 58
client software programs, 115
clip art sites, 29
clocks and telling time, 37
Collins, Stephen E., 142
coloring books, 28
comics, 73
compasses, using, 49, 50
composers, classical music, 38
compression software, 116, 117, 148

computer hardware for Internet connections, 109
Cone, Hannah, 48
configuring PPP setup
    Macintosh, 127–131
    Windows, 120–123
Congress, U.S., 51
connecting to the Internet, 109–131
consumer information, 29
content, evaluating Web, 11–21
control panel, network, 120–123
conversion, currency, 82
cooking. *See* food
copyright and the Internet, 89–90
Copyright Office, U.S., 89
countries, foreign, 82–83
crafts. *See* art
Crane, Nancy B., 17
currency conversion, 82
CyberGuide ratings, 13
    form, 20–21


# D

deserts, 42
    plants, 40
dial-up networking, 122–123
dictionaries, online, 31
digital music, 119
dinosaurs, 39–40, 41, 43, 44
discussion groups, electronic, 138–141
diseases, online information on, 31
dissection, frog, 42
distance learning, 108
documents, historical, 51
Dodge, Bernie, 16
downloading
    files, 145–149
    Web pages, 91
Duncan, Lois, 69


# E

earth science, 40
ecology, 42, 80–81
economics sites, 29
Eisenberg, Michael B., 1, 3
elections, 52
electronic discussion groups, 138–141
electronic publishing. *See* Web site creation
electronic resources, citation, 12, 16–19
e-mail, 133–138

e-mail–*Cont'd*
    attachments, 137
    exchanges, 32
    junk mail removal, 10
    postcards, 64–65
    software, 116, 117
embassies, 82
encyclopedia sites, 30
English. *See* language arts
environment, 40
evaluating Web content, 11–21
evaluating student research, 12
evolution, 39–40
exchanges, e-mail, 32
experts online, asking, 10–11
extensions, address, 133–134

# F

Fair Use Guidelines for Educational Media, 90
files
    compressing, 148
    signature, 137
    transferring, 144–149
filtering software, 107–108
financial information. *See* economics sites
first ladies portraits, 51
flags, 67, 83
    American, 53
    state, 51
flight activities, 76–77
food. *See also* nutrition
    chuck wagon cooking, 56
    costs, 63
    Native American, 55
foreign countries, 82–83
foreign language sites, 30–31, 83
fossils, 41, 43
Frank, Anne, 47
freeware, 116–118. *See also* software
French cave art, 28
frogs, 42, 67
frontier, American, 55–58
fruit flies, 45
FTP (file transfer protocol), 144–147
    software, 116, 117
fun sites, 66–68

# G

games, 39, 67

gardening, 42, 81–82. *See also* plants
general resources, 25–26
geography sites, 49–50, 64
geologic history, 39–40
geometry, 74–75
George, Jean Craighead, 70
Gettysburg Address, 48
GIF software, 158
gold rush, California, 56
government sites, 50–52
grading student research, 12
graphics, 29
    Web, 158–159
graphing, 75
    calculators, 37
greeting cards, online, 65
Gregg, Josiah, 56
guestbooks, 159

# H

Hamilton, Virginia, 70
health information, 31, 40
Herskowitz, Scott, 89
Hiroshima, 63
Hish, Jerry, 73
historical documents, 51
history, 46–49, 53–59, 63, 64, 83, 84
Holocaust, 53, 54
home page creation. *See* Web site creation
homework help online, 59
Horton, Moses, 49
House of Representatives, U.S., 50
Howe, Julia Ward, 59
HTML (Hypertext Markup Language), 160–174
    adding links, 164–165
    background colors, 167–168
    beginning and ending tags, 160–161
    e-mail links, 167
    headers and line breaks, 163–164
    image tags, 161
    indenting text, 167
    reference guides, 159
    tables, 168–169
    tags, 173–174
    text size, 165–166
Hubble Space Telescope, 77
human body, 31
Hurst, Carol, 33

# I

icons, computer, 29
illustrators, 32
images, computer, 29
immigration, 52
inaugurations, presidential, 51
Indians, American. *See* Native Americans
information access
    Big6 Approach, 1–15
    WebQuest approach, 16
insects, 40, 45, 63
intellectual property rights, 89–90
international affairs, 82–83
Internet
    access, 109–115
    browsers, 91, 95, 116, 117
    connection, 109–131
    copyright and, 89–90
    logging on, 126, 131
    service providers, 110–112, 123–125
Internet Scout Project, 26
inventions and inventors, 42, 58
Irvine, Joan, 72
ISDN (Integrated Systems Digital Network), 112–113

# J

Jansen, Barbara, 13
Javascripts, 159–160
Jefferson, Thomas, 83
Johnson, William H., 46
journalism, 83–85
junk mail removal, 107

# K

karaoke, online, 38. *See also* music
keyword searches, 8–9
kid safe search engines, 9–10, 108. *See also*
    online safety
King, Martin Luther, Jr., 46

# L

LAN/WAN, 113
language arts sites, 32–35, 68–74
language sites, foreign, 30–31, 83

law resources, 50, 51, 52
Lear, Edward, 33
Lee, Sang T., 89
legislation resources, 50, 51, 52
Lewis, Bill Dallas, 72
Li, Xia, 17
libraries and the Internet, 107
Libraries, Presidential, 51
Lincoln, Abraham, 47, 48
listservs, 138, 139
    Big6, 3
    Scout Report, 27
literature sites, 32–35, 69–71
local area network (LAN), 110, 113
logging on to Internet
    Macintosh, 131
    Windows, 126
logic problems, 38

# M

maps, 49–50
    Civil War, 48
Marcy, Randolph Barnes, 58
materials science, 42
math sites, 35–38, 40, 41, 63–64, 74–75
McLachlan, Karen, 19
measuring, 38
Medieval studies, 53
meta-search engines, 10
midi files, 119, 160
migration, wildlife, 63
MLA (Modern Language Association) style guide for
    citing electronic resources, 17–19
MMDS (Multichannel Multipoint Distribution
    Service), 115
modems, cable, 114
money sites. *See* economics sites; currency
    conversion
monitoring software, 107–108
Montanaro, Ann, 71
Monticello, 83
Mormon Trail, 58
Multichannel Multipoint Distribution Service
    (MMDS), 115
multicultural education, 54–55
multimedia, 87–88, 119–120
*MultiMedia Schools* magazine, 26
museums, 28, 44
    American Museum of Natural History, 39–40
    Holocaust Memorial Museum, 54
    International Horse Museum, 56

museums– *Cont'd.*
  Louvre, The, 28
  Miami Museum of Science, 78
  Museum of Westward Expansion, 57
  National Portrait Gallery, 55
  Royal Tyrrell Museum, 44
  Science Museum of Minnesota, 75
  Smithsonian, 44
  Tenement Museum, 52
music, 38–39
  Civil War, 49
  digital, 119
  electronic, 160
mythology, 54–55

# N

Nash, Ogden, 34
National Archives, 57
National Park Service, 51
Native Americans, 54–55, 57
natural history, 39–40, 41, 43, 44
natural language searches, 6–8
nervous system, 43
netiquette, 98
Netscape Communicator, 91–95
network control panel, 120–123
networking, dial-up, 122–123
networks, 110–113
Newbery Award, 34
news, 83–85
news streaming, 116, 117, 149–150
newsgroups, 140–141
nutrition sites, 31. *See also* food
Nye, Bill, 40

# O

online greeting cards, 65
online safety, 97–108
online scavenger hunt, 68, 85–87
optics, 43
Oregon Trail, 56, 57
organizer, assignment, 13–15

# P

Page, Carter, 89
paleontology, 39–40, 41, 43, 44

paper airplanes, 76–77
Parks, National, 51
PDF (portable document files), 119
Pero, Carlos A., 28
photo analysis guide, 22–23
photography
  Civil War, 49
  immigration, 52
physical education sites, 39
physics, 40
Pinchbeck, B.J., 59
Pinkwater, Daniel, 70
planets. *See* astronomy
plants, 40, 42. *See also* gardening
  fossil, 43
plug-ins, 118–120
  audio, 119–120
Poe, Edgar Allan, 34
politics. *See* government sites
pop-up books, 71
portable document files (PDF), 119
portraits, Presidential and First Ladies', 51
postcards, e-mail, 64–65
Powell, Sam, 36
PPP setup
  Macintosh, 127–131
  Windows, 120–123
prescription drugs, online information on, 31
Presidential Libraries, 51
presidents, U.S., 50, 51, 52
Pringle, Catherine Sager, 55
probability, 41–42
problem solving, 1–15, 43
publishing, electronic. *See* Web site creation
puzzles, math, 36

# Q

queries, search engine, 6–9

# R

Radio Days, 73
radio programs, classic, 73
rain forests, 42, 80–81
rating form, Web site, 13, 20–21
reading, 32–35, 68–74
reference activities, 85–87
reference sites, general, 30
research on the Internet, 1–23, 59
  Big6 Approach, 1–15

research on the Internet–*Cont'd.*
    WebQuest Approach, 16
research reports, 12
Revolutionary War, 53
Ross, Betsy, 53
Rothman, David H., 89, 90
rubrics, 13
Rylant, Cynthia, 70

# S

Sackman, Gleason, 26
safety, online, 97–108
Santa Fe trade route, 56
scavenger hunt, online, 68, 85–87
school Web pages, creating, 155–174
science, 39–45, 76–82
    African Americans in, 46
    biology, 63
    earth science, 40
    ecology, 80–81
    flight activities, 76–77
    materials, 42
    optics, 43
    physics, 40
    rain forests, 80–81
    space, 77–78
science fair ideas, 44
Scott, Newton Robert, 48
Scout Project, Internet, 26, 27
screensavers, 29
sculpture, 28. *See also* art
search engines, 5–10
    kid safe, 9–10, 108
    meta-search, 10
Senate, U.S., 63
senses, human, 42
shareware, 116–118. *See also* software
Shirk, Cynthia, 38
signature files, 137
Sivin, J.P., 90
smilies, 137–138
social studies sites, 45–59, 63, 64, 82–85
software
    client, 115
    compression programs, 116, 117, 148
    e-mail, 116, 117
    filtering, blocking, and monitoring, 107–108
    freeware, 116–118
    GIF, 158
    graphics, 158–159
    guestbooks, 159

music, 119
    shareware, 116–118
    Web, 90–95
    Web page creation, 160
space, 40, 43, 77–78
space program, 43, 44, 62
sports, 39, 84
stamps, 47
Stanton, Cady, 59
starting points, Internet, 10
states, U.S.
    flags, 51
    geography, 49
statistics, 41–42
Stine, R. L., 71
study sites, 59
style guides for citing electronic resources, 17–19
suffrage, women's, 59

# T

tags, HTML, 160–169, 173–174
task definition, 5
Tecumseh, 55
teleconferencing, 151–153
    software, 116–118
telling time, 37
Telnet, 117, 118, 142–144
templates, home page, 169–172
Templeton, Brad, 89, 90
Terrell, Mary Church, 59
Thompson, Jim, 57
time, telling, 37
Tippecanoe Creek, battle at, 55
Todd, William, 55
tourist information, 82
Towell, Emily, 56
Trail of Hope, 58
transferring files, 144–149
translators, online, 30–31
travel information, 82, 83
tropical rain forests, 42, 80–81

# U

U.S. Copyright Office, 89
U.S. House of Representatives, 51
U.S. Senate, 63
underground railroad, 47
United Nations, 51

UNIX files
    compressing, 148
uploading files, 146–147
URLs (Uniform Resource Locator), 142
Utah history, 58

# V

Valley Forge, 53
vice-presidents, U.S., 52
videoconferencing, 108, 116
virology, 44
visual literacy, 22–23
volcanoes, 45
voting, 52, 59

# W

Walker, Janice R., 18
Walker, Nick, 79
WAN (Wide Area Network), 110, 113
weather activities, 78–80
Web Buddy, 90
Web pages
    capturing, 91–95
    downloading, 91
Web site creation, 74, 155–174
    adding links, 164–165
    background colors, 167–168

    beginning and ending tags, 160–161
    e-mail links, 167
    headers and line breaks, 163–164
    image tags, 161
    indenting text, 167
    software, 160
    tables, 169
    template, 169–172
    text size, 165–166
Web site rating form, 13, 20–21
Web software, 90–95
WebQuest approach to Internet research, 16
westward expansion, 55–56, 64
White House, 52
Whitman, Narcissa, 57
Wide Area Network (WAN), 110, 113
wild birds, 68
wildflowers, 81. *See also* plants
wildlife, 41, 44, 53. *See also* animals; wild birds
Willard, Nancy, 98
women
    Civil War, 48
    history, 59
    suffrage, 59
World Wide Web, 141–142
writing, 72–73. *See also* language arts

# Z

zip files, 148

# Web Sites

## A

ABC News, 83
Abraham Lincoln Online, 47
Access Excellence, 39
Across the Plains in 1844, 55
Adobe Acrobat Reader, 119
Advice from William Todd—1846, 55
Afro-American Myths and Fables, 45
ALA (American Library Association) Resolution on Filtering Software in Libraries, 107
Alice's Adventures in Wonderland, 32
All of the Embassies of Washington D.C., 82
AltaVista, 6
Amazing Bubbles, 74
Amazing Insects, 63
Amazon Interactive, 80
America Dreams, 16
American Civil War Home Page, 48
American Memory Collection, 16, 22, 49, 52–53, 87–88
American Museum of Natural History, 39–40
American Presidency—Grolier Online, 50
American Treasures, 48
Anarchie, 117
Animation Grove, 29
Anne Frank Online, 47
Armadillo, 98
Around the Web in 80 Minutes, 107
Around the World in 80 Clicks, 82
Art Teacher Connection, 27
Artifacts of Assassination, 48
Artsedge, 28
ArtsEdNet, 28
ArtServe, 28
ask an expert, 10–11
AskAsia, 54
Ask Jeeves, 6
AT&T 800 Toll-Free Internet Directory, 85

Athena, 40, 78, 79
A to Z Weather Index—USA Today, 78
Aunt Annie's Craft Page, 28
Aunty Math, 35
Aurora Page, 40
Authors and Illustrators Who Visit Schools, 32
Avery Kids Sticker Buddies, 65
AVI, 69
Aviation Education, 76
Awale: The Art of Africa Game, 46

## B

B.J. Pinchbeck's Homework Helper, 59
BAD (Basic Aircraft Design) Web, 76
Banph, 66
Bare Bones Guide to HTML, 159
Barnyard Buddies, 66
BasketMath Online, 35
Beanie Babies, 66
Ben and Jerry's Fun Stuff, 66
Beneath the Calamites Tree, 43
Betsy Byars, 69
Betsy Ross Home Page, 53
B-Eye, 40
Bibliographic Formats for Citing Electronic Information, 17
Big Busy House, HarperCollins, 71, 72
Big6 Approach, 1
Bill Beaty's Amateur Science, 40
Bill Nye the Science Guy, 40
Billy Bear's site, 29, 65, 66, 159
Biography, 47, 87, 88
Bison Company, 55

Blue Dog Can Count, 35
Blue Mountain Arts' Electronic Greeting Cards, 65
Blue Squirrel, 91
BMG Classic World Composers, 38
Book Stacks Authors Pen, 32
BookRead, 32
Boston Globe Online, 84
Boyce Thompson Southwestern Arboretum, 40
Boys' Series Web Page, 33
Britannica Online, 30
Bubble Geometry, 74
Bubbles—Exploratorium, 75
Bubbles—Science World, 75
Buffalo Soldiers of the Western Frontier, 56
BugWatch, 40
Build the Best Paper Airplane in the World, 76
Build Your Own Mars Pathfinder Spacecraft Model, 77
Building Rubrics, 13
Busch Gardens Sea World, 44
Butterfly Web Site, 81
Butterfly World, 81
By Popular Demand: Votes for Women, 59
Byzantine and Medieval Studies Sites, 53

## C

CakeWalk Home Studio, 119
Caldecott Award Page, 33
California, As I Saw It, 56
California Gold Country Highway 49 Revisited, 56
California State Department of Education, 106
Carlos' Coloring Book, 28, 887
Carol Hurst's Children's Literature Site, 33
Cartoon Mania, 73
CBC 4 Kids, 66
CBS News, 84
Cells Alive, 40
Census Bureau, U.S., 86
Children's Book Council, 33
Children's Literature Web Guide, 33
Chuck Wagon Cooking, 56
Civil War Maps, 48
Civil War Women, 48
Classical Music Files, 160
Classroom Internet Server Cookbook, 142
CNN, 84
Colgate-Palmolive Kid's World, 31
Color Landform Atlas of the United States, 49, 86
ColorMaker, 159
Columbia Electronic Encyclopedia, Concise, 30
Commerce of the Prairies, 56

Computer Incident Advisory Capability (CIAC), 106
Concise Columbia Electronic Encyclopedia, 30
Concise History of Pop-Up Books, 71
Connectix, 151
CONVERT, WSFO Louisville, Kentucky, 80
Copyright and K-12: Who Pays in the Network Era?, 90
Copyright Clearance Center, 90
Copyright Fundamentals, 90
Copyright Office, U.S., 90
Cornell Theory Center Math and Science Gateway, 40
Cranes for Peace, 63
Crayola, 28, 66
Crescendo, 119
Cuisenaire Kid's Page, 35
Currency Converter, 82
CUSeeMe (videoconferencing), 51, 116
Custer's Civil War Command, 48
Cut and Paste JavaScript, 160
CyberAngels, 106
CyberBee, 65
Cybercitation in Hawaii's Schools, 18
CyberGuides, 12
CyberKid, 74
CyberNetiquette Comix
CyberPatrol, 107
Cyber Sitter, 107
Cyber Snoop, 107
CyberSound Studio for Macintosh, 119
Cyberteens, 74
Cybrary of the Holocaust, 53
Cynthia Rylant, 70

## D

Dan's Wild Wild Weather Page, 78
Daniel Pinkwater, 70
DataViz Products, 90
DC Comics, 73
Detroit Free Press, 85
Diary of Emily Towell, 56
Digital Links Newsletter, 27
Dinosaur Eggs, 88
Dinosaur Trace Fossils, 41
Dinosauria, 41
Directory of Scholarly and Professional E-Conferences, 138
Disney Cards, 65
Disney Music Page, 160
Distance Learning Resource Network, 108

DK Kids, 67
Donner Online, 56

# E

Earth Viewer, 77
Economic Resources for K-12 Teachers, 29
Educast, 116, 117, 149
Edward Lear, 33
Eisenhower National Clearinghouse, 41
Electric Library, 6
Electronic Crime Branch of the United States Secret
    Service, 106
Electronic Style … the Final Frontier, 18
Elementary Problem of the Week, 35
Elementary Science Program, 41
Ellis Island, 52
E-Mail Discussion Groups, 138
Embassies, 86
The Embassy Page, 82
Encarta, 30
Encarta Schoolhouse, 46
Encyclopedia.Com, 30
Encyclopedia Mythica—Native American
    Mythology, 54–55
Endangered Species, 41
Energizer Bunny, 65
English Teachers' Web Site, 33
Enhanced CUSeeMe, 151
Enough is Enough, 106
ePALS, 32
Eudora, 117
Eudora Lite, 116
Evaluating: Grading and Scoring, 13
Explorer—Lesson Plans and Curriculum, 41–42
Eye on the Universe: The Hubble Space Telescope, 77

# F

Faces of Science; African Americans in Science, 46
Fairland Elementary School—Montgomery County,
    Maryland, 156
Fall Colors in Missouri, 42
A Family Friendly Internet, 106
FBI Internet Safety Tips, 105
FEMA for Kids, 78
Fetch, 117
50 States of the United States, 49

Filamentality, 160
Finding Your Way with Map and Compass, 49
First Nations Histories, 55
Five Senses, 42
Flags of All Countries, 83
Food Guide Pyramid, 31
Foreign Languages for Travelers, 30, 83, 85
Franklin Science Institute, 78
French Ministry of Culture French Cave Paintings, 28
Frog Dissection, 42
Froggy Page, 42, 67

# G

Games Kids Play, 39
Garfield Online, 66
Geometry Problem of the Week, 36
GeoNet Game, 49
Getting Around the Planet, 86
Gettysburg Address, 48
Giant Panda Facts, 12
GifBuilder, 158
Gif Construction Set, 158
Girls' Series Web Page, 33–34
Global Grocery List Project, 63
Global SchoolHouse, 61
Global SchoolNet, 61
GraphicConverter—Macintosh, 159
Graphic Station, 159
Graphing Calculator Main Page, 36
Great Paper Airplane Challenge, 76
Greentown Elementary School—North Canton,
    Ohio, 156
Grolier Interactive, 30
Guide for Educators, Kathy Schrock's, 26

# H

The Habitat of the Panda, 12
Hall of Presidents, 51
Hallmark, 65
Halloween Midi Page, 160
The Harlem Renaissance—Encarta Schoolhouse, 46
HarperCollins Big Busy House, 71, 72
Headbone Zone, 67
HealthTouch Online, 31, 87
The Heart: An Online Exploration—Franklin
    Institute of Science, 42

Historical Documents, 87
Historic Paper Dolls, 53
Historic Valley Forge, 53
History of Pop-Up Books, 71
History of Tecumseh and Tippecanoe, 55
History Place, 53
History/Social Studies Web Site for K-12 Teachers, 53
Home Page Template, 169
Home Team—Math, Baseball & The San Francisco Giants!, 36
Homework Helper, 59
Hopkinton Middle and High Schools—Contoocook, New Hampshire, 156
Hot Mail, 134
Houghton Mifflin Math Central, 36
House of Usher: Edgar Allan Poe, 34
How a Book is Made, 71
How to Make a Pop-Up, 72
How to Use a Compass, 50
Humongous Entertainment, 67
HyperStudio, 119

**I**

I*EARN (International Education and Resource Network), 61–62
IAT Infobits, IAT, 25
Icon Mania, 29
ICONnect, 10
Images of the American West, 57
Indonesian Tropical Rain Forest, 80
Infoseek, 8
Infoseek: Stock Quotes, 86
Inkspot, 72
Inquiry Almanack, 42
In Search of the Oregon Trail, 57
Intellectual Property in the Information Age, 89
Interactive Knee, 42
Interactive Mathematics Miscellany and Puzzles, 36
Intercultural E-Mail Classroom Connections, 32
Internet Explorer, 117
Internet Pizza Server, 36
Internet Public Library, 34
Internet Resources for Music Teachers, 38
Internet Watch Dog, 108
Invention Dimension, 42
Investing for Kids, 36
Invite an Author to Your School, 34

**J**

Jan Brett, 69
Jan Brett Postcards, 65
JavaScript World, 159
Jean Craighead George, 70
Join Us on a Prairie Tour, 12
Journey North, 63
A Journey Through Art with W. H. Johnson, 46
Judy and David Page—Online Songbook, 67
Judy Blume, 69
Junk Mail Removal, 107
Juno Mail, 134

**K**

K-5 CyberTrail Multicultural Curriculum Resource, 54
K-12 Acceptable Use Policies, 98
K12Net, 141
Kathy Schrock's Guide for Educators, 26
KidCafe, 62
Kid Klok, 37
KidLink, 62
KidNews, 34, 83
Kid Power, 34
KidPub, 74
KidsConnect, 10, 59
Kids Food CyberClub, 31
KidsHealth, 31
KidsQuest Rain Forest, 80
KidZeen, 74
KidzPage, 34
Knowledge Adventure Encyclopedia, 30
Knowledge Adventure Kids, 67
Kodak Picture Postcard, 65
Kodak Picture This, 65
Kristy's Desktop Creations for Kids, 29

**L**

The Labyrinth: Resources for Medieval Studies, 53
Learning Page, Library of Congress, 87–88
Legislative Resource Center, 50
Lesson Plan for How to Make a Rainstick, 80
Letters and Journals of Narcissa Whitman, 57
Letters from an Iowa Soldier in the Civil War, 48
Le Weblouvre, 28

Librarians Guide to Cyberspace for Parents and Kids, 107
Liftoff to Space Exploration, 78
List of Lists, 138
Listz, 139
Lois Duncan, 69
Looney Tunes Karaoke, 38
Lview Pro—Windows, 159

# M

M&M Math, 75
M&M Project, 75
M&Ms Line Plots and Graphing, 75
M&M's Studios, 75
Magellan, 10, 108
Making a Weather Station, 78
MapBlast, 50
Map Machine—National Geographic, 50
Mapmaker, Mapmaker, Make Me a Map, 50
MapQuest, 50
Mars Pathfinder, 77
Martin Luther King, Jr., 46
Martin Luther King, Jr. Tribute, 46
Math and Science Gateway, Cornell Theory Center, 40
Math and Science Pavilion, 37
Math Baseball, 37
Math Forum, 37
MathMagic, 63
Mathmania, 37
Matt's Script Archive, 159
MEGA Math, 37
MetaCrawler, 10
Miami Museum of Science: Making a Weather Station, 78
Microsoft NetMeeting, 117
Microworlds: Exploring the Structure of Material, 42
MidLink, 74
Mighty M&M Math, 64
Missouri Botanical Gardens, 42
MLA-Style Citations of Electronic Sources, 18
Monarch Watch—Butterfly Gardening, 81
Monticello—Home of Thomas Jefferson, 83
Moses Horton, 49
Mr. E's Home Page, 37
Mr. ShowBiz, 47, 87
Mr. Smith's Fifth Grade Research Reports, 12
MSNBC, 84
Multicultural Pavilion, 54
MultiMedica Schools Magazine, 26
Museum of Westward Expansion, 57

# N

Nabisco Kids, 67
NASA Quest Project, 62, 77
NASA SpaceLink, 43, 78
National Center for Missing and Exploited Children, 105
National Council of Teachers of Mathematics (NCTM), 37
National Geographic Dinosaur Eggs, 88
National K-12 Foreign Language Resource Center, 31
National Park Service, 51
National Portrait Gallery: Native Americans, 55
National Science Teachers Association, 43
National Women's Hall of Fame, 59
Native American Foods, 55
NCSA Telnet, 118
Nebraska Center for Writers, 72
Nesting Falcons, 10
Net-Happenings, 26
NetMeeting, 151
Net Nanny, 107
Netparents.org, 106
Netscape Navigator, 116, 117
NetVet, 10
Neuroscience for Kids, 43
New York, NY, Ellis Island—Immigration, 52
Newbery Award Page, 34
Nine Planets, 77
Noodles, 72
Northern Lights Planetarium, 43
Now Politics, 18
Nueva School MLA Style Interactive Forms, 18
Nutrition Café, 31

# O

Observing the Weather Today, 79
Odyssey of the Mind, 43
Office of the Clerk, U.S. House of Representatives, 50
Official Peanuts Web Site, 67
Old Timer's Page, 54
OnlineClass, 62
Online Dictionaries and Translators, 31
Online Educator, 27
On-line Legislative Resource Center, 50
Online Songbook, 67
Optics for Kids, 43
Oregon-California Trails Association, 57
Oregon Trail Interpretive Center, 57
Overland Trail, 58

# P

Pacific Bell Education First Knowledge Network Explorer, 106
PageWorks—Kitty Roach, 29
Paper Airplane Aerodynamics, 76
Paper Airplane Hangar, 76
Paper Airplane Science—Lesson Plan, 77
Paper Airplanes—Quick and Simple, 76
Paper Dinosaurs, 43
Patrick Breen's Diary, 58
PE Central, 39
Perry-Castaneda Library Map Collection, 50
Photo Site Presents Influential African Americans of the 20th Century, 47
Pitsco's Ask an Expert, 11
PKZip, 148
Poetry and Music of the War Between the States, 49, 88
Portraits of Presidents and First Ladies, 51
Postcard Geography, 64
Poudre High School—Ft. Collins, Colorado, 156
Prairie Traveler, 58
Prem's Fossil Gallery, 43
President, 51
Presidential Inaugural, 51
Public Schools of North Carolina, 38
Pythagoras' Playground, 38

# Q

Quest Project, 62, 77
QuickTime, 119, 120

# R

R. L. Stine, 71
Rain Forest Action Network, 80
The Rain Forest Workshop, 81
Rain or Shine, 79
Read In, 34
RealPlayer, 120
Reproduction of Copyrighted Works by Educators and Librarians, 90
Reuters, 84, 87
Rocket Mail, 134
Roget's Thesaurus, 85
Royal Tyrrell Museum, 44
Rulers, 86

# S

Safe Kids Online
Science Learning Network, 44
SCOOP Adventure Page, 35
Scout Report, 27
Scriptito's Place—Vangar Publisher, 73
Sea World Busch Gardens, 44
Secret Service Electronic Crime Branch, 106
Selected Civil War Photographs, 49
Selective Learning Network, 63
Senate, U.S., 51
Seussville, 35
Seven Wonders of the Ancient World, 54
Sevloid Guide to HTML, 159
Shack's Page of Math Problems, 38
Shockwave, 120
Silly Billy's World, 72
Smithsonian, 44
Sony Artist Information, 39
Space Calendar, 44, 78
Space Curriculum—Athena, 78
SpaceLink, 43, 78
SPiN Goodies: Multi Guest Book, 159
Sports Illustrated for Kids, 84
Stamp on Black History, 47
StemNet Science Fair Home Page, 44
STOMP, 81
Street Cents Online, 29
Student Portfolios & Self-Assessment Rubrics, 13
Student Use of Netscape as a Research Tool, 13
StudyWeb, 59
Stuffit Expander, 117
Surf Watch, 108

# T

T.W.I.N.K.I.E.S. Project, 44
TEAMS Distance Learning, 62
Teen Link, 74
Teen Voices, 74
Teens Court TV, 52
10 Big Myths About Copyright, 90
Tenement Museum—New York at the Turn of the Century, 52
Territorial Seed Company, 81
Texas Instruments web site, 38
Theodore Tugboat, 35
This Day in History, 84
THOMAS Legislative Online, 51, 87
Timbuktu Pro, 118, 151

Time for Kids, 84
Today in History, 84, 86
The Toucan Sam Rain Forest Encyclopedia, 81
Trail of Hope: The Story of the Mormon Trail, 58

# U

U.S. Census Bureau, 86
U.S. Copyright Office, 90
U.S. Historical Documents, 51
U.S. House of Representatives, 51
U.S. News Online, 84
U.S. Secret Service, Electronic Crime Branch, 106
U.S. Senate, 51
The Underground Railroad, 47
United Nations, 51
United States Holocaust Memorial Museum, 54
Unusual Paper Airplane—Using a Straw & Paper, 76
URLabs/I-Gear, 107
USA Today, 84
Utah: Then and Now, 58

# V

Vandergrift's Children's Literature Page, 35
Videoconferencing for Learning, 108
Virginia Hamilton, 70
Virology, 44
Virtual Flowers, 65
Virtual Fly Lab, 45
A Visit to Capitol Square, 88
VivoActive Player, 120
Volcano World, 45
Vote Smart, 52
Votes for Women, 59

# W

Wai'anae High School—The Island of Oahu, Hawaii, 156
Warner Brothers—Animation 101, 73
Warner Brothers Web Cards, 65
Weather Calculator, 79, 85

Weather Cam, 88
Weather Channel, 79, 85
Weather Curriculum—Athena, 79
Weather Dude, 79
Weather Folklore Lesson, 79
Weather Here and There, 79
Weather Underground, 79
Web Buddy, 108
Web Central—Government Information, 52
Web Mind, 38
WebQuest, 16
WebSpawner, 160
WebWhacker, 91, 108
Web Wizard—Windows, 160
Welcome to Pennington Seed, 81
Welcome to the Planets, 45, 77
Westward Ho!, 64
What You Should Know as a Parent, 105
White House, 52
Why Files, 45
Wild Birds Unlimited Bird Feeder Cam, 68
Wildflowers in Bloom, 81
Windows to the Universe, 78
Windy's Design Studio, 159
Wing Design and Aspect Ratio, 76
WinZip, 116, 148
World Book Encyclopedia, 30
World Factbook, 82
World Record Paper Airplane, 76
World Wide Web Frequently Asked Questions, 142
WS_FTP, 116
WSFO Louisville, Kentucky: CONVERT, 80
WWW Calendar Generator, 86

# Y

Yahooligans Countries, 83
Yahooligans search engine, 10
Yahooligans, 108
Yak's Corner, 85
You Can with Beakman and Jax, 45
Yuckiest Site on the Internet, 45

# Z

ZooNet, 10

# More CyberAge Books from Information Today, Inc.

### Uncle Sam's K-12 Web:
### *Government Resources for Educators, Students, and Parents*
**Compiled by Laurie Andriot**

*Uncle Sam's K-12 Web* is the only comprehensive print reference to federal government Web sites of educational interest. Three major sections provide easy access for students, parents, and teachers. Annotated entries include site name, URL, description of site content, and target grade level for student sites. Uncle Sam's K-12 Web helps children safely surf the Web while enjoying the many fun and educational Web sites Uncle Sam offers—and guides parents and teachers to the vast amount of government educational material available online. As a reader bonus, regularly updated information and links are provided on the author's Web site, fedweb.com.

**Softbound • ISBN 0-910965-32-3 • $24.95**

### Internet Blue Pages, 1999 Edition:
### *The Guide to Federal Government Web Sites*
**Compiled by Laurie Andriot**

With over 900 Web addresses, this guide is designed to help you find any agency easily. Arranged in accordance with the US Government Manual, each entry includes the name of the agency, the Web address (URL), a brief description of the agency, and links to the agency's or subagency's home page. For helpful cross referencing, an alphabetical agency listing and a comprehensive index for subject searching are also included. Regularly updated information and links are provided on the author's Web site.

**Softbound • ISBN 0-910965-29-3 • $34.95**

### K-12 Networking:
### *Breaking Down the Walls of the Learning Environment*
**Edited by Doris M. Epler**

Networking has become a useful tool as well as a way of organizing people, their work, and their resource needs—and this is especially true of schools and school library media centers. The chapters of this book address hundreds of real concerns educators have about implementing various types of networks in the schools.

**Hardbound • ISBN 0-938734-94-6 • $39.50**

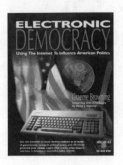

### Electronic Democracy:
### *Using the Internet to Influence American Politics*
### By Graeme Browning

Here is everything you need to know to become a powerful player in the political process from your desktop. Experienced Washington reporter Graeme Browning (*National Journal*, Center for Democracy & Technology) offers real-world strategies for using the World Wide Web to reach and influence decision makers inside the Beltway. Loaded with practical tips, techniques, and case studies, this is a must-read for anyone interested in the future of representative government and the marriage of technology and politics.

**Softbound • ISBN 0-910965-20-X • $19.95**

### Electronic Styles:
### *A Handbook for Citing Electronic Information*
### By Xia Li and Nancy Crane

The second edition of the best-selling guide to referencing electronic information and citing the complete range of electronic formats includes text-based information, electronic journals and discussion lists, Web sites, CD-ROM and multimedia products, and commercial online documents.

**Softbound • ISBN 1-57387-027-7 • $19.99**

### Great Scouts!
### *CyberGuides for Subject Searching on the Web*
### By Nora Paul and Margot Williams

Yahoo! was the genesis, the beginning of a noble attempt to organize the unruly Web. Years later, Yahoo! is still the beginning point for many Web users. But as the Web has grown in size, scope, and diversity, Yahoo!'s attempt to be all things to all subjects is often not enough. This guide discusses the growth of Web-based resources, provides guidelines to evaluating resources in specific subject areas, and gives users of subject-specific resources the best alternatives—carefully selected by Nora Paul (The Poynter Institute) and Margot Williams (*The Washington Post*).

**Softbound • ISBN 0-910965-27-7 • $24.95**

### Finding Images Online:
### *ONLINE USER's Guide to*
### *Image Searching in Cyberspace*
### By Paula Berinstein

While text research has been done at the desk for years, finding images has traditionally meant either relying on professional stock image houses or engaging in long, often fruitless searches. Today, cyberspace is exploding with millions of digital images, many of them in the public domain. With a personal computer, a modem, and this book, you can learn to efficiently evaluate, search, and use the vast image resources of the Internet and online services plus powerful databases designed specifically for image searchers.

**Softbound • ISBN 0-910965-21-8 • $29.95**

## The Extreme Searcher's Guide to Web Search Engines:
### *A Handbook for the Serious Searcher*
**By Randolph E. Hock**

"Extreme searcher" Randolph (Ran) Hock—internationally respected Internet trainer and authority on Web search engines—offers straightforward advice designed to help you get immediate results. Ran not only shows you what's "under the hood" of the major search engines, but explains their relative strengths and weaknesses, reveals their many (and often overlooked) special features, and offers tips and techniques for searching the Web more efficiently and effectively than ever. Updates and links are provided at the author's Web site.

**Softbound • ISBN 0-910965-26-9 • $24.95**
**Hardbound • ISBN 0-910965-38-2 • $34.95**

## Finding Statistics Online:
### *How to Locate the Elusive Numbers You Need*
**By Paula Berinstein**

Need statistics? Find them more quickly and easily than ever—online! Finding good statistics is a challenge for even the most experienced researcher. Today, it's likely that the statistics you need are available online—but where? This book explains how to effectively use the Internet and professional online systems to find the statistics you need to succeed.

**Softbound • 0-910965-25-0 • $29.95**

## The Essential Guide to Bulletin Board Systems
### **By Patrick R. Dewey**

This book details the setup and operation of bulletin board systems, which are interactive computer databases. There are chapters on hardware and software selection, software applications for personal computers, operational problems, and working with the World Wide Web, as well as examples of bulletin board system operations. These chapters are followed by invaluable resources such as a vendor list, Internet service providers, distributors, consultants, bulletin boards to call, and bulletin board system resources on the Internet.

**Hardbound • ISBN 1-57387-035-8 • $39.50**

## Teaching with Technology:
### *Rethinking Tradition*
### Edited by Les Lloyd

This latest informative volume from Les Lloyd includes trailblazing contributions from the 1998 "Teaching with Technology" conference. The presentations—by some of the leading experts in the field—are divided into four categories: Cross-Discipline Use of Technology, the Web as a Tool in Specific Disciplines, Technology Management for Faculty and Administration, and Techniques for Enhancing Teaching in Cross-Discipline Courses. If your college or university needs to be on the cutting edge of the technology revolution, this book is highly recommended.

**Hardbound • ISBN 1-57387-068-4 • $39.50**

**Teaching with Technology**
*Rethinking Tradition*

Edited by Les Lloyd

## Administrative Computing in Higher Education
### Edited by Les Lloyd

With the expansion of campus-wide information systems and networks comes the advent of administrative computing: the use of networked systems by administrative personnel. Educators and campus administrators directly involved in the planning, building, and management of administrative computing systems in colleges and universities discuss models of data sharing across systems, upgrading administrative software, selection and expansion of computing systems, and much more.

**Softbound • ISBN 1-57387-007-2 • $39.50**

## Design Wise:
## *A Guide for Evaluating the*
## *Interface Design of Information Resources*
### By Alison J. Head

> "Design Wise *takes us beyond what's cool and what's hot and shows us what works and what doesn't."* —Elizabeth Osder, The New York Times on the Web

Knowing how to size up user-centered interface design is becoming as important for people who choose and use information resources as for those who design them. This book introduces readers to the basics of interface design and explains why a design evaluation should be integrally tied to what we trade cash for and fire up for everyone else to use—in settings of all kinds and sizes.

**Softbound • ISBN 0-910965-31-5 • $29.95**

## The Internet Unplugged: *Utilities & Techniques for Internet Productivity...Online and Off*
### By Michael A. Banks

*The Internet Unplugged* is the first complete guide to the online and offline "extras" every Windows user needs to make productive use of the Net. Author Michael Banks not only demystifies these software tools, he shows you where to find them, offering tips and techniques for using them effectively. Learn all about:
- File compression and archiving programs
- Add-ons and plug-ins for sound and video
- Data encryption and decryption utilities
- Programs for building and managing a Web site
- Installers and downloaders

**Softbound • ISBN 0-910965-24-2 • $29.95**